Dolphin Odyssey

By
Aros Crystos

Copyright

Copyright © 2023 by Radhaa Nilia, Radhaa Publishing House All rights reserved. No part of this book may be reproduced in any form or by any electronic or mechanical means, including information storage and retrieval systems, without written permission from the curator, except for the use of brief quotations in a book review.

Table of Contents

Forward From Radhaa Nilia 1
From The Authors Desk 3
Chapter 1: The Calling 5
Chapter 2: Beverly Hills 17
Chapter 3: The Awakening! 25
Chapter 4: The Dolphins 27
Chapter 5: Telepathic Transmissions 31
Chapter 6: Interspecies Communication 35
Chapter 7: Chap In the Language of the Stars 37
Chapter 8: The Cosmic Heart 41
Chapter 9: Sweet Realization 43
Chapter 10: Timelessness Through Radiation 45
Chapter 11: More Light: More Responsibility 49
Chapter 12: Dimensional See-Through! 57
Chapter 13: First Transmissions 59
Chapter 14: Nature is Your Birthright 63
Chapter 15: Hale Bopp! 67
Chapter 16: Transmissions from the Star Command 73
Chapter 17: Magnetic Resonance 77
Chapter 18: Portal Beyond Human Consciousness 81
Chapter 19: The Sun Speaks 83
Chapter 20: Hale Bopp Continues 87
Chapter 21: Abundance Transmission 91
Chapter 22: Crystalline Energies 95
Chapter 23: Greetings from Destination Unknown Reality 97

Chapter 24: *Holograms!* *99*

Chapter 25: *More Hale Bopp Transmissions* *101*

Chapter 26: *What is Energy?* *103*

Chapter 27: *Last Transmission & Acceptance* *105*

Chapter 28: *Orchestra of the Universe* *109*

Chapter 29: *Glide Gracefully into the 5th Dimension* *115*

Chapter 30: *The Elementals* *119*

Chapter 31: *Sonic Codes* *123*

Chapter 32: *Nothing is as it seems* *127*

Chapter 33: *Multidimensional Soul* *133*

About The Author *139*

Forward From Radhaa Nilia

Dolphins, those enchanting creatures of the sea, have forever held a sacred place in the depths of my heart. From the early days of my childhood, when my dear grandmother would whisk me away to aquariums in the vibrant city of San Francisco, a surge of exhilaration would course through me whenever I found myself in the presence of these majestic beings. In their company, an inexplicable love seemed to emanate, transcending the limitations of human expression.

As destiny wove its tapestry, I found myself residing on the sun-kissed shores of Malibu, where the daily spectacle of watching dolphins gracefully dance in the ocean became my cherished form of entertainment. And on one extraordinary afternoon, an extraordinary encounter unfolded before my very eyes. Seated on the porch, accompanied by my beloved mother, our gaze was fixated on a solitary dolphin gracefully traversing the waters. It was an uncommon sight, for dolphins are known to thrive in harmonious pods. Yet, as if choreographed by the universe itself, a magnificent whale materialized, mirroring the dolphin's intricate movements with ethereal elegance. We were captivated, spellbound, and an inexplicable sense of wonderment washed over us.

Then, like an unexpected symphony, laughter erupted from our beings, simultaneously bursting forth from our souls. A wave of euphoria engulfed us, as if we had ascended to ethereal heights, weightless and brimming with boundless joy. In that extraordinary moment, I found myself propelled to dance around the house in sheer bliss, questioning the very nature of my existence, so filled with effervescent lightness. The dolphin and the whale, in their wisdom, had bequeathed upon us their sacred sonic codes, illuminating our world with vivid hues and transforming it into a technicolor paradise. It was as though we had stepped into the embrace of the fifth dimension, an indescribable experience that forever etched itself upon the tapestry of my life.

And thus, when destiny led me to encounter Aros, a mystical soul entwined with the dolphins and their sonic codes, I knew that the time had arrived for the profound messages of these benevolent beings to be unveiled. Within their luminescent presence, they carry an extraordinary reservoir of light frequencies, offering a guiding beacon to humanity. This book, dear reader, opens the doorway to their secrets, inviting you to embark on a journey of discovery, with an open mind and an open heart, to embrace the exquisite messages that ripple through its pages.

In the grand tapestry of our future, we shall come to fathom the immeasurable significance of these benevolent beings, particularly the dolphins, and the profound contributions they have bestowed upon humanity. Their intelligence, surpassing our own in many ways, invites us to humbly learn from their wisdom and grace. Let us embrace the divine union between our species, fostering a symbiotic relationship that will illuminate the path to a brighter, more harmonious world.

Within the pages of this book, prepare to embark on an odyssey of enlightenment, as the dolphin's sacred messages echo through the depths of your soul, forever altering your perception of our interconnectedness with the natural world. Open your heart and mind, for the dolphins' wisdom knows no bounds, and their love, like an eternal melody, shall serenade your spirit, resonating within you long after the final words have been read. In love for humanity and the eternal dance of life, may the profound wisdom and boundless love of the dolphins forever illuminate our path. With heartfelt gratitude and reverence, Radhaa.

From The Authors Desk

Dear Readers! I have been on the spiritual path my entire life, and since I was already aware of many things at a very young age, my mind was more curious about what life is all about and who I am. What is life, and what is death? Then the ordinary, like making money, careers, and relationships. This curiosity took many forms, visions and dreams, and experiences. Energies, vibrations, and starships and how they flew in and out of dimensions became my entertainment. Receiving transmissions from my multi-dimensional soul became natural, and the more I received, the more I wanted to know and remember. This book is a transmission from many different realities and dimensions of how it opened me up and uncovered the various layers to allow me to remember again. finally, I am a divine multi-dimensional being, and we are all part of one divine consciousness, playing with itself as the world and millions of universes. Allow yourself on these pages to see yourself as a unique possibility and to rediscover the wondrous being you truly are. With deep respect!

CHAPTER 1
The Calling

I have always felt that this world and all the actions performed have been backward. Or like in the reverse mirror. This led me, at an early age, in Sweden to look at my immediate surroundings and people's actions with a question. What is this all about, and why am I here? Who am I? What is the purpose? What and where do I go when I die? I was very preoccupied with these questions, so much so that my father once said, you should be more concerned about living people than dead ones. Did not satisfy my curiosity and instead opened me for more questions. At a very young age, I faced many people dying in various ways, and I had had my quota of funerals for this life. Otherwise, my teenage years were filled with inside rebellion and trying to understand why the school was so important, so I challenged my teachers with all sorts of questions, and no one could give me an answer I could accept. To put it bluntly, I was rather bored and asked questions about Everything and soon found out that even my parents and teachers were as clueless as I was. I knew one thing, though, that I somehow knew that I knew and could not access what that was. Very disturbing. It was like having the key to a treasure and could not find the keyhole. So, during the night, when I was supposed to sleep, I played with my imagination and a very active mind.

Then I started to have all these exciting experiences around starships and how they flew in and out of different dimensions. I recall flying them at times, which was a huge contrast from not being able to add numbers in school to explain the science of dimensional travel. It added a new dimension to my questions that were much more exciting, and I became aware of life and its possibilities in another way. So much so that it was pulling me to choose to quit school at sixteen and set out on my quest. Another trigger was when I was 19 years of age, and my parents had moved to Germany. When I came to Germany for the first time, I felt at home for the first time here on this planet. My mother, at a very young age of 50, was diagnosed with cancer, and it took her a year to waste away from being a beautiful woman to a skeleton. To witness this at 19 was something of a major wake-up call I could not escape, and I realized the thin veil between life and death, a few years later I had a question about something and for some reason I called upon her and she came to me in a vision, she was radiant and had achieved a very elevated state of consciousness, after that moment I let her go. I was like a character in a Greek play, and the gods witnessed my odysseys, who certainly did their part to challenge me all the Time. I am not talking about it briefly. No, through most of my life. I discovered that when I dared to ask the right questions, life would be gracious and point me in the right direction by meeting guides and masters that empowered me to continue until I met my destiny in my Guru Baba Muktananda. This eventually would lead me to the dolphins and their divine messages for me and being asked to be a Dolphin Ambassador.

I still had many years of clearing and challenges to master before that could happen. My first Spiritual teacher was Elizabeth Haich, well known for her bestseller Initiation, and I met her in Zurich, Switzerland, in 1979. I was at a major crossroads in my life and lived in the mountains of Berner Oberland in the quaint village of Gstaad, a playground for the planet's elite. What was I doing there? If you ever choose to read one of my books, Time Is Promised To No One. You will find out. After reading her book, I called her out of the blue and felt this energy rushing through me out of excitement, and listening to her voice; I felt like I was plugged into an electrical outlet. After agreeing to see me, I took the train to Zurich, and when I encountered her, she was eighty-two years old and a spiritual powerhouse. The first thing she said to me was, if you had seen me as a young child, you would have recognized me. I visited her several times until she felt it was Time for me to be on my own, and with the parting words," Everything you are looking for is inside of you," at that moment, that was not what I wanted to hear, and of course, she was right. That set off a trigger of a very potent past lifetime in Germany, more specifically, during 2nd world war, where I was a German pilot and a spy for the resistance and died when I was about twenty-five and when the plane went up in flames I went into ecstasy, and I was liberated. Another part of that vision was that, once, I had to catapult out of my burning plane, and as I did, my soul left my body and hoovered underneath it and took it very gently down to the ground and then reentered my body, and my body was saved and unharmed that time.

That vision opened me up to remember something I was not quite ready to embrace. This was like a precursor of what was to come. It also explained my love for Germany growing up in Sweden, why my wall was decorated with photos of military planes, and why I loved to build them from a kit. It also explains why I feared flying as a young man. The memory was not of the state of liberation; instead, it was the physical aspect of going down in flames. Another important lesson from Elizabeth Haich was that I had shared my love and fascination with other dimensions, ships, civilizations, and beings. She told me you must let it all go for now. Otherwise, your ego will use it against you, and you may not be able to complete what you came here to do, and know what I did for over twenty-five years. I recall the last time I saw her in Zurich, it was a grey rainy day, and she said I have two tickets to see Dr. Josph Murphy, a very famous author and lecturer, as he was giving a talk in Zurich that same day. She said I am not going, and you must go. I did, of course, with a feeling of sadness as it was the last time I would see her, as she had made that very clear. The talk was fascinating as he was talking about galaxies and other civilizations and beings; I was excited to meet him afterward. As I was standing in line with many other people, one of his assistants qualified the question you might have. I was told everything you are looking for is within yourself. I never met him; it was clear that I was on my own for now and had to have the attitude of a spiritual warrior. In the meantime, my father had died as well. I was truly alone with myself until I met my Guru, so I did forget about my galactic self and all that it represented for me, and when the time was ripe for me to reconnect with that part of myself again, I did so in an ashram in upstate New York with my next teacher, my Baba Muktananda. In 1979 I met a woman in Marbella-Spain, a famous psychic, and she told me I would meet a man with a dark complexion and that my entire life would change. In those days, I had a clothing boutique in Marbella, Spain, and a secret bank account in a Suisse bank on Bahnhofstrasse in Zurich. I had a charmed life, married to a gorgeous young German woman. We had the Boutique, a few horses, a nice place, and enough money, well invested in lasting this lifetime, yet with a nagging feeling. Everything was about to change; not because I was told, it was there my intuition had always been very powerful, even as a child, too close for comfort.

My guru had thrown out the fishing line, and I was hooked, slowly and very deliberately pulling me out of my comfort zone and preparing me for the next blow in my life before I was ready to meet him. In Gstaad a few years earlier, I had met Helen, my destiny and the symbol of unconditional love and the end of my old life, the high society of Europe among the wealthy and the noble ones. Yes, I was still married, and so was she. What happened? This encounter was destined to happen, and as part of my letting go, my fairy tale marriage ended. I had been there for a short ski vacation, and the hotel I stayed at was popular in the village. I had come down early in the evening for a glass of wine. It was crowded, and suddenly this handsome couple turned to me and said, you can sit here. I squeezed in beside them. She was very attractive in a red dress and long curly blond hair, and he looked like a distinguished gentleman. I was told that they were too early for a dinner party and decided to drop in and have a drink; she was from Sweden, so we had that in common, and he was from Switzerland. They introduced themselves as Helen and Jean and lived in Geneva, they let me know after not too long, they had to leave, and he said, I have to go down to Geneva for a week for business, and if my wife is ok with it, can you take care of her? That question was like an echo from a distant time somewhere in the universe and would change and alter everything in my life. I looked bewildered at both of them and then at her and said, if Helen does not mind, it would be fun to do that, she had a curious look on her face as she said, great, we can speak Swedish for a week ski together. I learned that she had to be careful on the slopes as she had had a severe back injury from a water ski accident almost two decades ago.

One evening we were meeting at a restaurant, and I was playing with my crystal wine glass to make tones; as she walked in, time stopped, and I felt like a character in an epic love story. The week passed very quickly, and I was going to Germany to complete divorce procedures with my German wife's soon-to-be ex-wife. I had decided to stay one night in Zurich, and the phone rang. I did not expect any calls as no one knew where I was. I picked up and was silent, and then I heard a whispering voice, I am in love with you. That was the beginning and the end of my old life as I had known it and the beginning of my true destiny. The next year was like a roller coaster of emotions and feelings, a love I did not know was possible. We had not touched or kissed yet, and at the same time, we were like two flames merging, and those feelings were exquisite. We did not see each other much except here and there in Marbella, where her mother lived, so she came with her family to spend the summer. This was when Bjorn Borg was winning Wimbledon, so we used this as an excuse to be close together on the beach of Marbella Club to listen to the match on the radio. We were afforded one week together at the end of the year and a couple of weeks before she was to fly to China with her husband. We checked into the same hotel we had met a year earlier as Mr. and Mrs. We imagined we were married and did the things that a couple in love would do, quiet romantic dinners, walking hand in hand on the snow-covered pavements and even went inside a small church and just sat. Our intimacy took so many tender and beautiful forms, and we discovered what we felt for each other went far beyond human conceptualization; it was love not of this world, and in my book, Time is Promised To No One, Alexandra is based on her persona. A few months earlier, we also had a very intense encounter in Paris, and I was returning from Los Angeles with a stop over in Paris to meet up with her. She was there with her husband on a business trip. I was tired from jet lag and also very emotional, and I had done my best to forget her by dating a few other women in Los Angeles. One was the girlfriend of a Mafia Boss, and another gorgeous black woman who took me to a club where no white man was allowed. The dancing was incredible and the people wonderful. She asked me to stay and move in with her, for a moment I considered this a real possibility. My destiny made sure that did not happen.

The flight back to Europe was filled with screaming children and parents doing their best to keep them quiet, and every Hotel in Paris was booked as a big conference was taking place. I was exhausted and had managed to find a small Hotel in a part of Paris I did not cherish too much. The phone rang, and I did not know where I was and what time it was like a drunk person. I answered. Can you meet me later? I only have a few hours to spare so if you want to go shopping with me, you can do that. Her words were like a cold shower, and I was awake. We met at the Champs Elysees and stood on that crowded street in the afternoon, hearing the next fatal blow to my old life. I can not see you anymore. I did not need that, and I was upset and angry and felt this was not right and not the time and place for this. If you leave Paris today, I will meet you in Geneva in a few days when I return, and we can talk. Of course, I left. We had dinner at the hotel where I was staying, and we talked; she said, let's go back to your room and in the elevator, she said if you had said the wrong words, I would have left. We had a very intimate few hours, and then she said in a crying voice, I want to die with you. From a deep place within myself, I hear this voice; it is not time yet. Before she took the elevator down and out of my life in these bodies, she took my hands and looked into my eyes and said, you have so much strength; use it. Then she was gone. In retrospect, we had been like two children playing house as we sometimes imagined living together and planning a life, knowing it could never happen. We both during this year felt we were given these exquisite moments as a gift and that they would not last, it was like we tried to live our entire lives in a few short moments before time was up, and because we felt it, every moment became a special gift of grace and the intensity of we are running out of time. She later called me and said I feel complete. I have nothing more to wish for. The next day I was flying back to Spain, and she was on her way to China with a stopover in Athens. I am reading on the plane in the Herald Tribune that Swiss Air runs off the runway, a few hours later, back in Marbella, it is a beautiful autumn day, and it is still warm and sunny. I was glad to be back home, and I was thinking about her on her way to China, and I felt a glow in my heart. The next moment a woman of royalty approached me. Have you heard, suddenly, all the beauty of this day was replaced with a feeling of panic, and she confirmed they had both died on the plane in Greece? I started to cry from a place I did not know existed deep down below all concepts and ideas and as if something in myself broke and opened up to another part of my being, and the strange sensation came over me, and a love for God I had never felt before. It was confusing as it seems I would have experienced the opposite and at the same time, so lost and forlorn, and I looked up into the sky and saw some birds flying into the light between the clouds, and I realized that is all that has happened, she is in the light. This episode of my life was a game changer, and now I was ready to surrender to the next chapter of my old life. I did not want to go back to my place. I stayed at the Club for a week in my room with white walls and a candle lit and prayed for her to go into the light, and I was not going to hold her back. The net was closing in on me, and I was being prepared to meet my true and lasting destiny in my Guru Baba Muktananda. It states clearly in the Indian scriptures to be so fortunate to meet a true Master and Guru. All your karmas from this life and many others must be in perfect balance, neither negative nor positive.

That was exactly what was taking place, even though I did not understand it at that Time. I had lost all the money in a volatile stock market. As I mentioned before we had some very special and intense moments together, granted and bestowed by God's grace that the Time we spent together was His gift to us. Hot noonday in a parking lot in Marbella, I had a powerful vision and the message that we had been given this time, that we were not these bodies or minds and were divine spirits. I was crying as these words came pouring out of me, and then later, when I found out she had left this reality, something was severed within myself, and I could never again go back to full body consciousness. At that moment, something else happened.

Yes, I did die and was reborn instantly, and somehow as I mentioned, my love for God had never been stronger; I was simultaneously crying out of love and despair. You must remember I have never been a religious person, and yet God has, one way or the other been with me all along. He never let me forget what was important. These incidents opened my heart, and newfound creativity came pouring through me, yet I was still not quite ready to meet my master, a little more balancing of the karmas. I found myself back in Gstaad, and a dear friend let me stay in her sixteenth-century chalet while she was traveling and divorcing her husband. The year I was there, I did not speak, except going to the store, and I was faced with my inside demons and the very frightened imaginings they brought up to the surface. For the first time in my life, as far as I can recall, I was really scared during the night and slept many times with the light on. At the same time, my creativity was taking huge leaps, and insights into writing became my father and mother in those days.

One day my friend asked me if I would cherish a change of scenery, I was all ears, and she said, how about driving my red Ferrari to the French Riviera, St Tropez, where she had a house? In Time is Promised To No One, I go more into the details of this episode of my life, and it's worth mentioning that after months of meditating several hours a day and practicing the spiritual way of life, and thinking about

God all the time, I am speeding down the curvy and stunning mountain roads in Switzerland and France. I felt ecstatic for the First Time in a very long time and was grateful for my life. What else was in store for me? The next evening in the twilight light of the day, I heard from within myself, pull over! So, I did, and the voice climbed that little hill, and of course, I did, and in the distance, I saw this starship blinking, and I said, I am ready to go with you! Of course, that was not what I had been clearing my karmas for, so I could only gaze upon the ship and feel the longing in my heart and soul. All this also led me to the dolphins in Hawaii about fifteen years later. My life has been an adventure in consciousness to deepen my connection to my soul and be free again. My little trip to southern France became another stepping stone to letting go of my old life for now. I even had an opportunity to spend some time at the film festival in Cannes, and I have not been back since that Time in 1980.

My destiny was preparing me for the final blow to my ego and all its trappings. In Gstaad, several months earlier, I was skiing one day, and this man fell at my feet. I helped him up and took him to the chairlift back to the village. It turned out to be a well-known actor that will remain a secret. He was so grateful that he invited me to come to Cannes. So, he kept his promise and introduced me to his people, and I felt inspired to show him maybe the book Time Is Promised To No One that was not even close to finished. My dream was to make it into a movie. He did look it over and said," If you do the movie, I like to play the main character. My destiny was playing with me, and these feelings of God, my path, a movie, and Hollywood were somewhat confusing. The trap was closing. Sometime later, I found myself in Geneva-Switzerland, in a Hotel room, with no clue what I would do with my life, what direction to go, and what to do. I used to write down my dreams and interpret them immediately, even at 3 am, and staying in this Hotel was only temporary as I was running out of money. On the 2nd day there in the morning, I had so many vivid dreams, and I knew a message was in one of them! Which one was the question for me? My destiny knew the answer, so I called the airline and asked for the next plane to London. Remember those days when you could do this? I was told in 3 hours. When was the next after that? In a week! My mind was racing like the Grand Prix of Monaco, and I managed to shift gears, calm myself down, and look at the situation. I was ready to leap a faith and maybe have an opportunity in Los Angeles with my film. I knew intuitively I had to leave Europe. My Master and Guru were bringing me closer to him. Three hours later, I was on the plane to London and a quick stop overnight to catch a plane to Los Angeles the next day. You could buy an airline ticket for about $100 one way to Los Angeles. Life certainly was, in so many ways, so much easier. I landed in LA and became aware of the sign, being aware of pickpockets. I traveled with a very expensive suitcase and handpicked clothes from various countries that I still had in my belongings, such fun and one-of-a-kind pieces. I was on a business trip to Los Angeles about a year earlier. I had put together a real estate deal that could make me wealthy, and the mind is tricky, and had already created a positive outcome even before anything had happened. I would become a millionaire when this deal goes through and truly there was no real reason for it not to happen, except it was not my destiny.

    I stayed at the Beverly Wilshire in a suite for a few weeks. The deal fell through, and I returned to Europe and Spain. My luggage went through the first screening at the airport, and then I had to put it on a conveyor belt and pick it up by the exit. An hour or so! Still no luggage. I reported it missing. It never arrived and was never found again. I was thinking, after going through my emotional drama and vain hopes, that whoever took it, trust you will at least enjoy it, and then I realized it should be possible to sit down right now and meditate, and of course, I was at the airport and wanted to get out of there. I went to some friends in Newport Beach, and he and his wife said not to worry about it. We will find a way. He was a prominent businessman, and when I had met him in Gstaad years earlier, I was still very much part of a different world. Even then, my life has always been under the spell of spirituality. I was still on my odyssey. You may wonder what all of this has to do with the dolphins. You will come to discover all the incidents were like pieces of a giant puzzle and will fit perfectly together, and so what I am sharing has Everything to do with my encounters with the dolphin energy and their messages to me and this world of illusion. After a few days, they asked me to leave, and they felt uncomfortable with me always talking about God and spirituality. They took me to John Wayne Airport, and from there, I took a bus to LAX to look for a hotel and to find the people I had met in Cannes. I now had my dirty laundry bag, the clothes I wore, and $200.00 to my name. The final chapter was written that would end this part of the Odyssey. The only Hotel that answered on the board of hotels at the airport was Hotel Carmel in Santa Monica. They came and picked me up, and on Ocean Blvd, I saw a big blue tent on the beach, and I asked the driver, what is that? Oh, it's a yoga thing. I was intrigued and tired, and hungry. Oh, ok, my answer sounds interesting. My room was $70.00 a night. I paid for two nights and was left with $60.00 and a growling stomach. I went to a restaurant within walking distance from the Hotel. I had just ordered my food when I walked past a woman I used to know from San Francisco. We looked at each other, and she explained I was on my way home, and suddenly my car took me here. I have not been here before. We exchanged information, talked briefly, and decided to meet in a few days.

    The next day I went to look for the people I had met in Cannes and went to the Blue Tent. Nothing came out of it, and tomorrow I had to check out and was left with less than $ 40.00. I did not sleep well, and my dreams did not help much either. I still wore the same clothes I had had on the plane, and my Italian loafers with thin soles were not meant for walking on hard pavements. I took the Bus into Beverly Hills and am not a fan of any bus. I rather walk, and it was a bit too far to walk, so I did what I had to do. Out of habit, I was drawn to the last place I had stayed a year ago, Beverly Wilshire Hotel. The manager recognized and treated me from memory, having stayed in a suite for two weeks. I did not tell him my situation and asked if I could leave my bag there while I went to a meeting. He did not hesitate. I walked Beverly Hills streets with $35.00 in my pocket. Last year I went to any store or boutique and bought what I wanted without looking at the price. Closer and closer to my real destiny, and I could almost taste It. Late afternoon I was tired from walking and very worried and hungry. I had even asked someone I knew who owned a hair salon if he could give me a job, anything sweeping the floor, that is not your destiny, was his answer. I ran into two women I briefly had known. They told me about a European Hotel on the side street of Wilshire Blvd. Luckily it was only about a ten-minute walk, and it was a bright-colored colonial building almost standing alone in a cul de sac. Yes, we have rooms for $ 25.00 per night. I could not believe what I was hearing. My room was big with a bed, table, chair, and bathroom, even a black and white Television.

CHAPTER 2
Beverly Hills

I was very grateful for this room, even for one night, and I was destined to stay there for the next three months as my destiny was pulling me closer and closer. Many times during this time, I could feel how invisible energy guided me. I went through my bag, and to my surprise, I had left some of my jewelry in there, so the next day, I went to a pawn shop and got $200.00! Now I could stay for another week and still have some money for food. The next thing I did was walk a mile to find a laundromat to clean the few things I still had left. It felt great to put on clean clothes, and my inspiration came back to me, and I was eager to sit down and write about my current situation. A few days later, I come down into the lobby, and to my absolute surprise, I spot an acquaintance from my days in Marbella. He looks at me and asks, what happened to you? You must remember he had last seen me when I lived a very different lifestyle. Now I looked like one of the characters from Down and Out in Beverly Hills. I am sure you can imagine the look. I failed to mention that I still had one more object from my old life. A Santos Cartier Watch on my wrist, and when I bought it in Spain, I paid $3.500, and it was hand-delivered to me on a quick stop in Madrid on my flight from Malaga to New York. I was flying first class in those days. I even got to fly on the Concorde from Paris to New York, another tale for another time. He looked good, healthy and suntanned, and happy. The contrast was like night and day. He shared that he was returning to Spain after his Honeymoon in the Bahamas, and he added I always stay at this hotel when I am in Los Angeles. I asked him if he wanted to buy my Cartier Watch. No, he said! I know of someone who will. He took me to a friend in Beverly Hills who bought it for $ 800.00.

My destiny was to be kind to me and let me go out in style. Having had money in a Swiss Bank Account, I had a very comfortable life; at that moment, that $800.00 felt like more than I ever had before. So my tour of Beverly Hills started. For the next three months, I walked up and down the famous streets of Beverly Hills. I even applied for jobs, but no work permit, no job. I wrote a lot, had very real and powerful dreams in colors, and learned to interpret them. I dreamt in color and golf that I had grown up with, which now became a symbol for my spiritual quest. The hole on the green was the merging of the soul with the absolute and the golfball was the soul, the golf club the action, and the player the seeker as I dreamt of hitting the ball close to the hole. It inspired me and gave me the courage to continue. I also learned from studying some of Carl Jung's books about the symbols in dreams. I was dreaming that a turtle had hidden underneath my car and I used a shovel to help it come out, when I learned that turtle could mean subconscious mind, it made so much sense, that I was digging out all the hidden clues within that part of the mind, and of course, later on I realized that there is no mind as such it is all divine consciousness and at that moment it was very helpful. The dreams gave me an amazing insight into my adventure, and I knew I was where for a specific reason, giving me the energy and initiative to keep going. As charming and delightful as Beverly Hills can be, it started to get old and boring, and the allure left me after a month of walking around. This was not exactly what the Aborigines call a walkabout; Christmas was around the corner, the holiday season upon Los Angeles, and my money was running out. I recall my thin clothes did not protect me from the chilly December air and I tried to think warm thoughts to keep warm one day I was at the corner of Little Santa Monica Blvd and Rodeo Drive and at the light a woman in a Bentley stopped and I looked at her and longed to sit in her car and just be held nothing else. No matter what, I had decided to have about $140.00 left to repurchase a ticket to London. John Lennon was killed, and people asked me if I was his living spirit walking around. I never quite understood how people associated me with him, not just once frequently. I had befriended a waitress in the Restaurant Café Casino, and she had a few times invited me to her home to have a home-cooked meal with her and her son. She was like a guardian angel and often did not let me pay for my tea and croissant. She gave me the book I Ching, the book of changes. to read your destiny through coins.

Change, change was running through my mind. The change I had been waiting for was about to happen. Yet my patience and energy level were dwindling rapidly, and I had difficulty staying positive. A few days earlier, I had come into my room and lightly hit the television for it to work. On the screen, I saw a short footage of an Indian man in an NBC peacock jacket, and it was shared that he had walked over India for 27 years and was now in Los Angeles giving lectures and grace. I know how you feel, I said to myself. I have walked for three months. The holiday season passed, and I was down to just about the money to get back to Europe, and the change I had felt was now a mild tumult in my mind. I went to my friend in the Restaurant and said, "I am leaving. I cannot take it anymore; this drives me up the wall. She answered, where are you going? I shrugged my shoulders, and she looked at me with a smile and said, before you do something foolish, let me introduce you two to these ladies. You know they talk like you, and they come here all the time. I was hesitant and curious at the same time. She introduced me to three ladies in their forties and well-dressed. Looked like successful businesswomen. I do not recall how I started to share about Elizabeth Haich, my teacher from Switzerland, and they were excited that I had met her and wanted to know more. They explained when they went to India to spend time with their Guru, Elizabeth Haich's book Initiation was a must-read. Why do you not come and meet our Guru? I interrupted, in a blue tent in Santa Monica, they looked perplexed, and I explained that three months earlier, I had gone to the Tent and was told it was closed for a few days for a special program. They were visibly excited and said, come tonight, and we will introduce you to him, and then I realized he was the man the psychic had seen in her reading about me in Marbella. I find it very interesting how close I had been to him for the last three months and yet until it was time, I would not meet him on the physical plane I used to think truly that opportunities in life came when the right place and the right time came together, I failed to see that the most important factor was that I had to be the right person and that was often the missing link in not just my life, in many others as well. Part of life seems to be to become the right person.

They said it's your destiny to meet him, and you are fortunate to have this opportunity. I took my beloved bus. I am being ironic here. The Tent was filled with people that looked more like they belonged at some celebrity event in Hollywood, not in a tent with an incense smell and candles and typical Indian music at the same time, the energy was lovely, and people looked happy. My dear ones, I want to clarify that Meeting my Guru was part of meeting the Dolphins ten years later. There is no way I could have understood and been able to communicate telepathically with them if I had not gone on this odyssey; as you will come to see later, the dolphin energy to be understood, self-effort, and willingness to surrender was a must. Later, I received one of the first messages in 1994 on a beach in northern California. "Where there is true love, shapes, and forms disappear and left is only our smile" That message could be from an Indian Scripture and has tremendous meaning and to understand this, the first part of this odyssey was completed this evening in the Blue Tent, and the next adventure was now waiting. I was introduced to Swami Muktananda, or his followers called him Baba, in the darshan line, and he blesses people with Peacock feathers with the aroma of sandalwood. Here I was in front of the man I had met energetically a few years earlier, I felt welcomed, and that was nothing special. The simple food we had later was filled with lifeforce and energy, and my friends said, come back tomorrow. The next morning, I woke up wondering what I should do. If I stay another night, my ticket to London will be used up, and then I heard myself shouting, I am not giving up now. That is not why I spent the last three months there. I returned the same evening and was told I could stay like so many people worldwide and get a job. I have no permit I shared, no problem. We are well-liked, and people trust us. I Registered to stay with the little money I had left. It lasted me another two weeks with their special prices as they had rented several hotels along Ocean Blvd for the thousands of visitors worldwide. My hotel was the same one I had stayed at three months earlier; with the difference, I was to stay with five other guys in one room with bunk beds. Somehow, I got a job painting high-end condos in Westwood with other people from this group. I am not a house painter, and to paint these million-dollar places inside and out was testing my skills in karma yoga. Do your best, and surrender the result. One evening I came up in the darshan line to be blessed.

For the last week, I had studied people and asked many questions that I did not understand what this was all about; I had recognized that Baba was a man of God and, at the same time, what was my role in this? Why am I here? Standing in line, I asked myself, Baba, I am unsure why I am here; please help me understand. He hit me with the feathers, and I fell to the floor, enveloped in a piece I had never before felt or experienced, and I did not want to stand up again. However, I was blocking the lane, and as a drunk person, I stood up not very steadily, and then I heard this voice within me booming. This is how you are, this is what you have been looking for and I felt I was stoned on divine love. I had never taken drugs, yet stoned was the word I used, and I looked at Baba. He was like an infinite ocean of grace and divine love. I said to myself, whatever you have, I want it, and I was ready to do whatever it took to maintain that state of bliss. Later, I learned that he had parted the veil for me to show me my true essence, and with that, the real work began. I had managed to make enough money to stay for at least a month and that allowed me to have more awakening experiences. One night I awoke and felt that my heart was going to leave my body, my roommate's called out to repeat the mantra Om Namah Shivaya, the initiation mantra, baba used and I was repeating it as fast as I could and the next month I did not eat, I felt terrible and the very thought of food would make me want to throw up and sometimes I managed to eat some crackers and yogurt, meeting Baba I was already thin and now I felt like a skeleton and my only refuge was to try to read Play of Consciousness, one of Baba's books about his own experiences on his path before enlightenment, I read one page and fell asleep and during that month I managed maybe to read 2 chapters, in the middle of this I tried to go to one of the evening programs and someone approached me, saying," you are so lucky" I looked at him perplexed as I felt so awful still, he said, you have received shaktipat and I have been around Baba for a few years and you just arrived and he was visibly happy for me and yet wondered why i had received this precious gift so soon. In retrospect, I now understand what he meant. After about a month I started to feel like eating again and after the evening program, I had a green salad, the first real food in a month, and as I was putting the food into my mouth, I was removed from my body consciousness and saw how someone was feeding my body and it had absolutely nothing to do with me and the food dropped into an empty vessel with a light sound.

A month later the tour with Baba moved on to the Ashram in upstate New York and I had been sent with the advance crew a month earlier. When Baba arrived I was told to get a job as until now I had been offered to work and do a lot of seva, selfless service, and my food and accommodation had been taken care of. Now I had to find a job, I still had no work permit, and even so, it was a huge challenge of course. Grace helped me to find another painting job at a summer camp for rich children who wanted to study acting and directing. The many buildings had to be painted and freshened up and beds and other types of furniture moved around to accommodate the young people. When the morning chant started at 7 am, I started to walk for an hour and a half to get to my job and be on my feet for another 8 hours and then walk back again. After a few weeks of this another person from the Ashram with a car started to work there as well, so I had a ride. I never wanted to attend the evening program and be late and come after

Baba had been seated in his chair and all these following months, if I was late he was late, and the miracle of Grace was showing me many things and deepened my understanding about the Guru discipleship and its subtle workings. One evening I started to cry and I looked at Baba in a very crowded room with over a thousand people and asked from within myself, please take me home. I felt he stared at me as if to say, you asked for this, now let's see if you can take it. The saying, be careful what you ask for, was not present, and from that moment on the real work had begun I can say without any hesitation that I could never have mastered the next 30 years or so and the chipping away at the ego without Baba's grace and allowing me to have the right understanding so I could learn and keep going.

CHAPTER 3

The Awakening!

Maybe eons of time had passed for this moment to present itself. I know I had to walk the path to one day realize that there never was a path to walk. That was, about 3 decades later, to finally realize who I truly am. A divine multidimensional being, I have had powerful insights into my true nature as consciousness and countless challenges to break down my ego during this odyssey. Baba said! It's like your ego is being pulverized between two stones, and if you can take it, you will emerge this radiant jewel. Since this book is about the dolphin messages, I will not go into the tribulations I had to go through, and that is what the dolphins told me. We know the tribulations you have gone through.

At the same time, my dear ones, I think what I have shared with you so far has great validity as I have walked the path and understood and experienced that to remember who I truly am, God bestows three gifts a human body, the longing to be free and the master to show you the way. You will see that some of the dolphin messages are like the scriptures and can elevate your consciousness. Of course, dolphins are conscious breathers, which means they are aware of every breath they take; otherwise, they would drown. An interesting fact is to live in water and still breathe consciously to stay alive. Baba's lineage is Siddha Yoga, the supreme yoga, and another guru in the lineage must appoint the Guru, and then they bestow shaktipat to their followers. It's how the kundalini energy is awakened and then guided by the Guru. The candle within you is kindled by the Guru's grace and guided from deep within your heart and soul. The end of that journey is liberation. An interesting aspect is that when a master leaves their body consciously, they use one of the 72 million nadis in the subtle body or energy channels thinner than a strand of hair. The Sushumna nadi is the one they use to travel up the spine and merge with the absolute. The dolphins breathe through this Nadi, which explains why they are so conscious and use their breath consciously. I am sharing this because I have always looked upon the dolphins as divine masters in the Ocean, and without knowing how I know it has been confirmed one way or the other what the dolphins have shared with me through the years of interacting with them, in the open Ocean and energetically. The title of this book is Dolphin Odyssey, so it's not linear. I am weaving in and out of different realities and moving back and forth. Maybe some of you wonder about what I shared earlier about meeting my galactic consciousness again after 20 years, and it happened through Siddha yoga in the ashram upstate New York. The last place I would have thought my star connection would be established again, or it may be only my concept and not strange at all. You know the saying when something happens three times, pay attention; God wants you to hear something. Within maybe an hour, I was introduced to the book Bringers of the Dawn, a classical, Pleiadean music, and an article about my galactic family. The message was crystal clear. It's time to embrace this part of your destiny again. This was in 1994. A few months later, in Lake Tahoe, with a crystal-clear blue sky and white snow perfect for skiing, I took some photographs, and when I developed, a starship was right above me. A few weeks later, I received my first message from the dolphins. Here is the first message I received when sitting on Muir Beach in Marin County. I recall it vividly. I was at a crossroads and had just returned from the ashram in upstate New York and did not know exactly where to go and what to do.

CHAPTER 4
The Dolphins

I am sitting looking out over the Ocean, and suddenly these images and sayings are pouring through me, and at the end, The Dolphins? I mean, I was aware of Flipper and had liked him, and that was about the extent of my dolphin connection at that moment. That started an incredible part of my life that is still going on today. After several months of telepathic communication, I longed to swim with them in the open Ocean. By this time, I had heard about a woman on the Big Island who took people out to be with the dolphins. Let's call her Blue! I called her and was told she had two places left during Christmas. I arranged to fly to Maui as I knew someone with a place in the Bamboo Forest where I could stay. Arriving, I immediately called Blue and told her no flights to Kona and everything was booked. If you are meant to be here, you will, and apparently, I was because I took an early flight to Honolulu the next morning, was on standby to Kona, got the last seat, and took a taxi to the harbor, and the boat was just about to leave when I arrived. I had to leap onto the boat. Normally these tours take about 4 hours, and today something else was in store for us. On the boat were about 15 people, most of them from a group that had been to a spiritual retreat and wanted to culminate it with a dolphin swim. Now Blue was known to have an almost 100% encounter when she went out, and her captain was as well very well known, and the dolphins were very accommodating when he was out. This was the perfect place and time to be. The question was, was I the right person or the others on the boat? We saw some Bottlenose dolphins in the harbor on our way out into the blue Ocean. We meditated to call in the dolphins. We chanted, had lunch, snorkeled, and visualized following Blue's direction. 4 hours later, we were still out, and there were no dolphins. Blue said what are we still doing out here? We should be back by now. Not even the captain had an answer to this. We had been swept up in an energy field without linear time. We were back in the harbor eight hours later, feeling still in some powerful energy field. I would stay with Blue at her house, where she rented rooms. I had asked here earlier, out on the Ocean, if I could. She said sure, and the next moment she said, wait a minute, I am booked out already. She looked bewildered and shrugged her shoulders. We will make it work. She had a big American car with heavy doors, which is why I mentioned this. We left, and she was driving this road almost every day, and she took a wrong turn, and we knew something had happened earlier, and we were still in that energy field. She had to stop at the grocery store, and I was in the front seat, had opened the door, and was resting my bare foot on the side of the door. She came back and said let's go, I slammed the door shut with my toes in between, and she stopped. I opened the door, moved my toes, and said I am glad I do so much yoga. Nothing had happened. A couple of days later, I was back in Maui, and I awoke in the middle of the night and looked outside. The entire Bamboo Forest was dimensional, not flat anymore; it continues, and I know that is truly the way it looks once my limited perception is altered, and I kept absorbing it for at least 30 min. Then I am not sure what happened. The next day I was to go out with seven people on a sailing boat to be with the whales, the whales came right up to the boat, and the love I was experiencing from these beings was enormous. If I went in the water, I would not return. The same evening a white owl flew by me. You add it up, what happened on the boat, the bamboo forest, the whales, and now an owl? Something was happening, and I was not sure exactly what it was. A few days later, it was Sunday, and I was back in Marin County, working as a freelance Tour guide, and I had a schedule to bring a group to the wine country that morning. It was drizzling, and there was no traffic at 7 am. When I reached The Golden Gate Bridge, the engine died, and lucky enough, I had enough speed to roll over the bridge to the tool boot on the other side. With a clear message, do not think for a moment that you are returning to this life. We are showing you if you do. I rescheduled my group until the next day. It took me the whole day to get the car fixed. I had some tickets to Marine World in Vallejo, and a day later, I drove up there to talk with the dolphins.

The dolphins had just been fed on the other side of the pool, and I closed my eyes and asked from my heart. If these messages for the last ten months, including the trip to Hawaii, had a deeper meaning please show me so I know it has all been real. had not finished my thoughts. One of the dolphins did a 180-degree spin, darted through the pool, and jumped where I was standing so I could touch it on the head with the message that when one of us interacts with you, it represents all our species. Telepathically, it was explained to me that they had tested me to see how I understood their energy and shared that we have been with you all the time and were guiding you in Hawaii and all that happened. How do you think you escaped unharmed from the car door? They certainly had a valid point there. They then asked me to be one of their trusted Dolphin Ambassadors on the planet. I was stunned and willingly accepted, with the thought, oh, now I get to be with them all the time in the Ocean. Was I ever wrong?

Three months later, I was going to Hawaii to live and be with the dolphins. Somehow, I started my dolphin tours with some saved-up money and was very excited to be with my first group of 10 paying people, or at least they promised to pay me. The captain would not leave without his cost covered. We headed across the mid-channel to Lanai, one of the most dangerous passages on the planet. The weather could change in an instant. There are a couple of bays by Lanai where the dolphins come and play. No dolphins, people were a bit disappointed and took it well and enjoyed the Ocean and the sublime scenery. On the way back to Maui, we went slowly in the zodiac to get a glimpse of something. I was playing with the water with my hand, and suddenly three elder dolphins were by my side, looking at me with so much love and simultaneously teasing me and the message, when will you get it? Twelve years later, I got it. However, after that brief encounter, we had dolphins and whales galore all the time we went out. I had to learn a powerful lesson right away: if people took advantage of me and did not honor the agreement to pay, the dolphins were clear. You need to treat this as a sacred business. Otherwise, we will not show up. What a powerful life lesson that was.

CHAPTER 5
Telepathic Transmissions

To all the warriors: "Be aware of your thoughts and actions. Understand that you have already chosen to be part of the transformation, and fear has been like a fungus. With all the light penetrating the atmosphere, fear will be no more. Fear can only exist where ignorance is rampant and, in its wake, Chaos and lack of trust in yourselves. It's your opportunity to stand up for yourself and become part of the change as a warrior in love. Yes, we said "In love" because when you fall in love with life again, you will fight with the weapons of creativity, which is far more effective than any other weapon. A creative project like a movie or painting, writing, sculpture, or anything like that is so powerful that not even the most ancient weapons can destroy it, look back in time to the Pyramids and other such structures. They have survived thousands of years and have influenced the very thought patterns of humanity.

Here I want to include another message that is so appropriate for today's world. Truly it is not a question about battle because when fears are rooted out, what meaning do words like battle, ego, duality, jealousy, greed, and anger have? When misery has grown so strong that people are fed up and will not accept what they are being fed all the time, through the news and internet and other ways, then they are ready to make a difference and live out of that understanding, and that will establish courage rooted from deep within a person and when that surfaces with right understanding it like a tsunami sweeping the planet. Out of that courage, the warrior is born, and out of the actions of those warriors, the battlefield will be the truth. There are no winners or losers. The only ones that might lose are the ones not participating in the first place. They are only the tail of the monster of fear.

What is light? Light is awareness manifested through layers of particles because when consciousness becomes aware of itself in these particles, they vibrate, creating an image of light. We are encouraging you all to live more at the moment. All things then become quite clear and simple. When you slip away from the moment, you discover the old patterns that seem to loom in the shadow of your lack of trust and do not fully embrace that you are truly a divine multidimensional being. At the same time, it is wise to remember that nothing that does not carry the vibration of serenity, peace, love, and unity will ever again have any real power over you. It is always darkest before dawn. How magnificent and splendid is that light in the new dawn? The heart is again the reigning force of your life. This process is facilitated by the fact that the human consciousness is now shifting to the awareness that choice based upon the heart will only produce sweet fruits. In light of all this, everybody is being asked to take a stand for themselves and the entire galactic evolution.

Many of you have been following a golden thread of energy that was illumined eons ago. You will recognize that this energy has always been before you and behind you. As dolphins, we are tuned into your feelings and can pick up the subtle sensations deep within you. We are truly swimming in the infinite ocean of our divine consciousness. Life can be like a happy wave surging through the ocean by sun-filled shores.

Please, dear ones! Do not get entangled by dates and linear thinking; know that these messages are valid throughout time and space and beyond. Was my life all easy and charmed? As I mentioned earlier, being an ambassador does not mean always being with the dolphins in the ocean. It is more like the opposite, so while I am interacting with them, they infuse my energy with coded patterns for me to share with humans on land, so when it's time for me to leave, they make it abundantly clear. Go out and do your work! I never know exactly when they will call me back to infuse more messages, and at the same time, I am always in contact with them. When I return, they seem to clean and polish my energies exposed to much of the human drama, and it's nice to have that removed. I feel lighter and more Intune and more energy. Twelve years later, I was with a small group on the Big Island. It was a bit choppy, so it was not easy to see the dolphins, and a few of them came right up to me and said, now you got it. The question that had been stated all these years earlier had now been answered. I knew exactly what it meant, my consciousness had merged with them, and I was part of the dolphin pod consciousness. Which, through the years, has been manifested in countless ways. I will continue sharing the messages from the dolphins, not necessarily in order, because these messages are timeless.

In the third dimension, you live with the questions. In the fifth, you are the answer!

CHAPTER 6
Interspecies Communication

"Angels do not fly with their wings; they fly with their hearts."

It is time to feel welcomed in our play and embraced by our sweet radiance. No more separation. Our joy is your path as well. The gates to soar into ecstatic vibrations are now fully open and activated. In that vibratory matrix, mother nature will be part of your life. You will once again remember to see through the eyes of an eagle, fully aware and detached and yet grateful for what mother earth provides to sustain life. This also indicates that the sleeping warrior is being awoken and set free. He can be seen in his illuminative light. In his right hand, he holds a light wand that gives birth to the universe, and in his left hand, he holds a tender heart symbolizing the ecstatic body of the universe. Practicing simplicity and clarity are powerful attributes to develop during tumult and changes. In simplicity, the eternal flame of love is burning. In clarity, the heart is the moon of the universe. Remember that parts of your body have been the hiding place for the world of duality, so negative emotions and feelings are not stamped automatically as negative. Everything is instantly exposed and transformed when the light is crystalized in every cell and molecule. When simplicity and clarity are the messages in your creative endeavors, they become like powerful magnets that draw other souls swimming in the same blue ocean of consciousness.

The truth is always patient. It knows that the time for it to express itself is always perfect and aligned with the divine heart. Sometimes it will feel like the earth's gravity is making itself more present inside your body and that your entire physical body is being removed and reassembled. That is what is taking place to hold the matrix of being a multidimensional being. Your frame of reference is also being altered, and it is like you are learning a new language to express yourself. You will come to recognize that mother earth exists within you and you within her, and not only that, the entire universe and cosmos are within you as well. When interacting with us in the open ocean, be aware of our bodies and see them as a perfect vehicle to move in and out of different realities, and dimensions, and shapeshift. It is the perfect instrument to channel high frequencies, and because of that, it creates a flowing energy spectrum. This greatly facilitates our travels in and out of different dimensions. We understand that at times you will ask yourself, what has all of this to do with your life, and how will this contribute to the awakening of humanity? We like to remind you that your cellular system was designed genetically always to transmit and hold the truth and not be practically immobilized by manmade truth. At this point, it's worth understanding that the truth does not flow in one direction and instead bounces back and forth on its own, and this creates the sensation of direction when this is understood as light and nothing but light.

CHAPTER 7
Chap In the Language of the Stars

Light bounces back and forth, creating a matrix of the living web of divine consciousness.

Light travels through many layers of consciousness to shine like the stars in your night sky. What is perceived as the brilliant light of the stars is the shadow of the divine light. Now imagine! If you truly saw the light itself. What you perceive as the world is the play of shadows originating from the divine light. Look at this way for an inside revelation to be felt and experienced. It may have to travel through a multifold layer of forgetfulness to reach your conscious mind. You are both the light and its shadows. Everything on your path and the path itself is your creation. These messages from us are like love letters printed in the divine ocean of love. The vibrations of these messages can bring you to the clarity that to accept us and truly love us, you must as well respect other parts of nature and hear the song of the wind, feel the vibration of the trees and their longing to be understood, look at the universe of insects as an important part of nature and its divine purpose, in this way when you become a crystal clear mirror for this understanding than you know who we are. Then the trust that has been established will open portals for you in your consciousness.

Trust can be a tricky affair! A child generally trusts its mother to feed it; that trust must now be earned later in life. What took place to change this? When we teach our young ones to take their first breath and trust in that, we are simultaneously bringing the clarity that all life is connected and that unity runs through all this creation, creating an innate trust in life. In your human language, you at times hold so dear.

Where is that taking you? Where have your clever ways of communicating taken you? Where has that innate trust between humans gone? What are we showing you, and where are we taking you with our interactions with you? We are guiding you back to your intuitive trust and allowing it to be part of your breath. This is grounded in understanding who you truly are, a divine multidimensional being, and allowing that to shine inside you even during a moment of darkness. We suggest that you take this to heart and contemplate it.

Here is a question? When you observe the stars in your sky, do you allow them to shine, or do they do that themselves? Similar in communication, do you allow the truth to be present naturally, or do you once again have to earn that trust? This is not a mind game; this is vital for the human consciousness to start thinking and embracing this way of being. This will lead to the conclusion when the light is consciously present, even the most intricate questions in life will be easily understood. It's part of the sacred mystery. Living with and in the light and embracing our communication and messages to you are not separated. Your divine light allows all methods and symbols to be clear and easily understood. In that space, no more confusion, and because of that, many of you have once again rediscovered sacred geometry and many other ancient and sacred teachings that have been able to hold the light for eons. So, it's not that they bring you closer to the light. When the light is accepted within you, and you live from that clarity, all other teachings in that same vibration will make themselves known to you again. In a piece of material, the hidden shape is already present, depending on the artist's understanding, which will determine how well it is brought out into a visible form. Because of your light, you now can communicate and, at times, play with us, respect and love us in the understanding that our purpose is multifold all the time, and as dolphins, we still play a certain role in the water that must be respected and honored. That is part of why we choose to be here as dolphins in the oceans: the magnificent blue ocean is truly liquid light.

This is not a mystery! The mystery is part of the question. Take away the question, and you will see, truly see. We are not a science project and be aware of people trying to avoid their ignorance by explaining why we seem to behave in ways your formulas and numbers cannot validate. Let go of ignorance and be open to the possibility that who we are and what we do is beyond your current grasp, be humble and ask for the right understanding. As an ambassador, you must always share and represent us so that people can be encouraged to widen their limited horizons about us and what we represent. One aspect of who we are is that we are travelers of the heart and multidimensional light workers, spinning an intergalactic web of divine consciousness. That can open the possibility that the mind and the heart must dance together in perfect balance and harmony to understand life. This must be achieved, especially in science; otherwise, no matter how much science thinks they know and have discovered, they are going nowhere. All that is achieved is more denial about your true nature. The whales shared with you that they would behave differently when they returned to the Hawaiian waters. What happened? Yes, as you recall, Aros, they started to sing out of the water. Your captain, a marine biologist and many years studying and interacting with whales in Hawaii and Alaska, was stunned and said, this I have never seen before. Part of their reason was to facilitate speeding up the frequencies to assist the planet in orbiting into its divine resonance. As an ambassador, you certainly have responsibilities to fulfill. That is also why we are infusing you with an understanding and vibration yet to be available to the masses. The saying With more light comes more responsibility is the absolute truth. Because of beings like Aros and others who have consciously chosen to become a beacon for the weary understanding of humanity, we can, through these messengers create a platform for more and more people to reach us and listen to us, so never underestimate these divine messengers and do not allow your limited understanding not to recognize their service to themselves and the entire planet. When you can honor and respect someone else for their wisdom without feeling you are less, you have attained a beautiful place within yourself. Another reminder that the solution to your questions can be found in your deeper feelings, so keep expanding your light and diving deeper and deeper, and the world as you have known it will start to vanish right in front of you. Left is always the only vibration of ecstasy. What you experience in your world, we are reminding you that that is such a minute particle in the overall picture, and everything is always a mirror in the kaleidoscope in the divine now. The moon appears round to man's eyes because of the inherent circle of love in the heart.

CHAPTER 8
The Cosmic Heart

The cosmic heart is once again beating in tune with your awakened awareness. We, the dolphins, whales, and many of your star families, have been waiting and preparing for the human family to be able to vibrate with us and be part of The Galactic Federation of Light worlds again. As more and more of you are now embracing this simple truth and consciously letting go of the appearance of duality and separation in various levels of understanding, we all assist each other all the time. The sacred clown will again be understood as the sacred truth, and all answers will be revealed in the laughter. Your lives are being aligned with the grace and stillness of the oceans. It's wise to let go of all questions that may confuse you, and it's time to embrace the ever-present answers within your multidimensional being. Also, remember every question serves its purpose depending on where you are and understand. Now this will eventually take you to a different depth of your being and there to trust the answers without the questions. Sounds like a contradiction. You are now accessing a world where the impossible becomes possible again. We also wanted to remind you about the whales and their divine purpose and share with you the great fortitude to listen to the singing of the whales that contains so much of the understanding of the sacred pathways. Our dolphin hearts and our entire energy field prepare your physical and emotional bodies and the range of your cellular systems to expand so that you will vibrate in sweet ecstasy in your unlimited beingness. The light and expanded awareness that comes with that will dissolve any trace of false expectation that has kept you from embracing and living in the fluidity of the moment. You will see that any truth must be an experience before it manifests as a truth. The knowledge is in the experience. More poetically, on the petals of the flower of wisdom within yourself is inscribed, all answers are contained within the eternal moment.

CHAPTER 9
Sweet Realization

This will also lead to the clarity and sweet realization that your life will become like ours, sweet and spontaneous, and that opens you up to live in a state of sweet surprise at any moment, and your life will be seen and realized as an innocent play. Such a heart is filled with divine memory, and the sacred chamber of such a heart has the power to transform broken hearts into dancing hearts. Some of the mysterious and sacred work we have been doing with the whales in the ocean is that we have magnetized a certain vibratory frequency that will maintain the sacred singing of the whales to be heard in the womb of the oceans even when the whales are physically not here anymore. This will be such a discovery that your science community must open to another part of their mind, as their methods cannot explain this. In short, what will be understood is that the oceans are the true walls of humanity. In many ways, the oceans will now become the next frontier. The focus on understanding the mystery within the ocean will once again be awakened, and many ancient answers will be revealed. This will be available for humanity, provided they change many of their destructive behaviors and become true Mother Earth stewardesses. This kind of wisdom and change has its vibratory expression. Anyone accessing it must change their vibratory level, even if it has always been possible. So now you can understand more. It is all about vibration. There are worlds within worlds in different frequencies, and once you understand that the divine is like a divine temple of frequencies without a beginning and an end, life, and death are still on the low scale of vibration. The oceans are divine blessings and gifts to the ones choosing to understand.

Aros Crystos

A new dawn awaits humanity as they change their vibratory level of understanding. It's the tree of life with its ripened fruits on ancient branches to be enjoyed and cherished, and as you taste the ambrosia of the fruits, it will bring into blossom the entire tree in your universal being. This is also the awareness and rising of Lemuria and Atlantis. That bright star will once again shine and guide the masses to the understanding this happens both inside and outside. That star had had many names through eons of time. Each time she arises again, she will give manifestation to a new being. You are that being, do not be shy in sharing this, as sooner or later, this truth must be recognized, and that is also why this timing is perfect at this time in your life. You will behold the splendor of the entire world as a ripened manifestation of the sprouting truth. Your entire body is being transmuted into a symbol of a sacred chariot. You will manifest more and more like us, like a magnet that will draw people and other beings into your spectrum of light.

CHAPTER 10
Timelessness Through Radiation

Aros, timelessness through radiation activation, is the true blueprint for your cellular memory. Let's give you an example of how to understand this. Radioactive! Two words, radio and active. In your language, radio is something you are broadcasting through and a tool to listen to various stations. The word active has many different meanings. Put it together. They take on a powerful tool to transmit information. This is part of the job your cellular system does. They continuously broadcast to all different parts of your body. They are the newscasters of your being. Your blood will pick up the news and as well distribute the news to other parts of your being. The cells also receive the information from your mind via the emotional channels and your nervous system. Your cells also receive input from your brain, which is part of your mind. Your brain is tuned into your heart, and your heart to mother earth, the Earth to the central sun in the Sirius star system. So, whatever happens in the central sun affects the earth, affecting the human heart, brain, and cells. We are mentioning this as you become more multi-dimensional. It is important to recognize these patterns. These messages are also part of the activation of what we shared with you, how what happens in the central sun creates a chain reaction inside your body and outside the physical Universe. You know you will be able to understand that the eternal truth is always flowing through your multidimensional being, and now you can tune it to the wavelength it is transmitting from. A way to keep this awareness fully activated is to practice what we share with you throughout these writings, trust in what we share with you, and allow that trust to motivate your actions. It also assists you in tuning into your telepathic abilities, which does not only mean being able to read other thoughts, but more importantly, it allows you to tune into the intergalactic heart of the Universe and your multidimensional being.

True abundance is a state of being! Let those words penetrate deep within your being, and they will also open portals. It is wise and important that when all this information is being absorbed and digested, please make sure you are kind to yourself, honor and respect the adventure you embarked upon, laugh, and dance.

Our smiles are forever engraved on your divine heart's temple walls. Surrender! What are you surrendering to? We are surrendering to the mystery of our lives and celebrating that surrender. We are celebrating the birth of the divine child within ourselves, and in that breath, we hear the music of I am that I am! Bubbles of laughter erupt from deep within, and we support Mother Gaia in her rebirthing and labor pains. We are rejoicing with her in her graceful transformation, and as we look at the sun, we behold her orb within our hearts. In the moon's cooling rays, we behold the ecstatic balance of the mind and heart. As we allow this understanding to blossom, we are also assisting ourselves in embracing our divine unfoldment and celebrating the female aspect of God once again. In her virtue, we recognize the spiraling ecstasy of the snake of realization; in that energy, we hear from the ecstatic whales I am, I am. We are diving deep down into the depth of our ocean and the sweet mystery of our soul. We arrive in the sea of magic, and in the center of her being, we behold ourselves as the divine mirror for the entire creation. Our hearts are beating to the rhythm of millions of universes. Finally, we are embracing unity in all things, and as we look at the blinking stars, we look to our souls in the sea of light-filled universes. We have now been released from the cocoon of fear and separation, and our wings will now take us to the top of ancient monuments erected in memory of our divine heritage. We thank you for the journey and fill ourselves with the elixir of gratitude. With our eyes, we now behold the ever-unfolding shine of our divine inspiration.

You are part of an unimaginable tapestry of light in the forever expanding and changing play of creation. Do not hold back your inspiring testimonial to a dying world of duality, and allow your awakening to be like a beacon and inspire others to follow. Even though you have walked in tumult, chaos, and fear, you have never been alone. Your daily life has been the stage and the university for all of you to become strong, gentle, and compassionate with yourself and others. The world, with all its challenges, is not your enemy. It's the opposite, and when you understand it is here to support and be your ally on your path, you have reached a great plateau to live from. Everyone is exactly where they need to be. It's foolish to compare yourself with others on the path. One of the pitfalls for humans is that as they advance in anything they do, they have the real tendency to measure their growth by comparing. It leads to nothing except more confusion and more disharmony between the mind and the heart. We know that many of you who will read these words in this book will wonder, these are the messages from the dolphins? Refrain from being confused by our form, tune into our energy, and know that truth can appear in many shapes and forms.

Some of you had had a clearing in your consciousness to be activated. In that energy, you pick up subtle vibrations from different beings in various dimensions. As Aros picked up the frequencies of the comet Hale Bopp, which is not a comet, it is an interstellar library from some of the highest light workers in the army of divine light workers. We, the dolphins, encouraged Aros to be attentive to the transmission coming to him. First, he hesitated and asked why I would pay attention to a comet. At the same time, he has been practicing trusting what we share with him, so he let go of the question and focused on the answers presented to him for ten days in 1997, where he received powerful insights from an ultrasonic wavelength. He had no clue at times what he was writing down, yet he followed the guidance and once again showed us why we had chosen him to be an ambassador.

CHAPTER II
More Light: More Responsibility

More light, more responsibility. Of course, as always, it is not the word so much. The energy behind the words is true communication and dynamic results. At this point, dear ones, we like to remind you all that as the waves in the ocean are always one with the ocean and can never be separated, in the same way, everything that we are sharing with you is only vibrations in the one divine consciousness, playing with itself as countless universes with countless manifestations and beings, we live in that understanding all the time, and that is what we teach our young ones as soon as they are born into the water. Why have humans completely and utterly neglected this and fed their young ones information that has very little to do with what we are expanding on in these writings, so you get caught up in that you must become something and strive to return to yourself again? How can you become something when you are already everything? You have created this amazing movie and are both the director and the audience. Once you are tired of all of this, you will naturally remember that part of the solution to recall to acknowledge that the female and male within yourself must merge again. All your physical attention to relationships is a vain attempt to achieve this in the physical world. Your fascination with us as dolphins is because we mirror something different for you. It allows you to be triggered to remember what we are sharing with you in a very natural way. You have heard this many times. You are truly the one you are looking for, and as you reconnect with yourself as angels and masters and star seeds, you are welcoming yourself back home to yourself.

We, the dolphins! The sacred clowns of the ocean and the radiant energy behind the radiant light offers salutation to all the warriors of peace and light. What is a sacred clown? An intricate way of releasing light beams through a clown's amusing ways and awareness. When the cells are infused with light in the form of laughter and joy, they vibrate at different frequencies. In that vibration, old and negative patterns are exposed and catapulted out of the system, similar to how a spacecraft moves into hydrospace by its creation of propulsion speed.

As dolphins and whales, we have become somewhat of a symbol for healing the way we use our sonar and our pure intent when we want to penetrate the densest matter and recreate it once again into flowing energy. That energy is not limited by time and space.

Right now, Aros, we are infusing your brain with electromagnetic images showing up as the words you are writing down, and at the same time, you are being taught how to hold and understand light in its holographic nature.

Remember! Truly light beings are only as bright as their image of themselves.

Hawaii is truly a sacred home for your soul. Even with all its changes, the gentle Tradewinds, the sun, the ocean, and the life force are healing for a turbulent mind. Sometimes when you are not seeing us in the ocean, be clear that we are all around you. As we have mentioned many times, it is important at times to tune into our energy field and perceive us in that understanding, and a lovely aspect of this is that with your feelings, you are sharing your heart and intent with us. In this book, we gently prepare you to glide gracefully into the fifth dimension if you like. The work you have done over the last twenty years spreading our message and energy to many places worldwide is changing the blueprint of human consciousness. Also, part of the work has been to create a new human species born out of the divine memory in the human soul. We wanted to remind you, Aros, that your commitment to serving humanity and the planet in this way will not go unnoticed when you least expect it; fortune will smile upon you.

The waters are sacred because of their natural honesty. Its inhabitants will naturally understand that inherent quality as well.

Music is one of the most powerful ways to connect and communicate and relate to each other. We are talking about vibration, like our sounds and the whales singing, you can call it music, and it's still a vibration since everything is made from vibration and frequencies. Imagine your body is like an orchestra; every organ is an instrument. Before you play in an orchestra, you must tune the different instruments to be in perfect harmony for the piece of music to be performed and cherished. If one instrument is out of tune, that will affect the entire piece. Your body is not different; every organ in its natural state vibrates in tune with the entire composition. When one of the organs is out of tune, it affects the whole body's well-being, which is how sickness happens. If the music is not in harmony, it causes stress to the listener, and when the organs are not in tune with the body's overall function, it also causes stress. That is partly why so many of you feel healed and nourished by interacting with us in the ocean. We are not healing you. We are creating a vibration that helps the body to heal itself. Your body is the greatest healer, provided you listen to it and trust its guidance. The mind created the body, so all healing starts with the mind.

Anything else is just a temporary distraction. Does not matter how you look at it. Stress starts with your thoughts. Your thoughts become your belief system, and that then becomes your reality. When science comes to this self-evident realization, sickness and a weak immune system will be something of the past. We are mentioning this for you to start thinking independently and become aware of yourself again, understand why you love us so much, contemplate this, and ask questions about anything you are impressed or influenced by. When you do, you take yourself easily out of the limited mind matrix and align with your cosmic heart. Then you will be living life instead of reacting to life.

Here is something to think about. In the dawn of time, life was precious. In the knowledge, it was a divine play. In ancient times life was less precious and had become the play of the learned ones, and later and today, it has become the creation of the ignorant. We suggest you contemplate this and allow it to show you something that will assist you in remembering your divine heritage. In the blueprint we brought to this planet, we have a formula that allows us to remember who we are when forgetfulness is rampant. That is another way we are assisting you. With us, you easily start to recall your divine blueprint. All the agreements that have kept you in the dark for thousands of years are now dissolving and part of the agreement to a certain degree. That causes upheaval and separation like never before. All the programming of fear and unworthiness surfacing from your subconscious mind to be fully seen in the light of your conscious mind. It's because the fear illusion is breaking into pieces and scattered all over your understanding until it finally destroys itself.

Only the truth can remain in the understanding that a human being is a combination of many starseeds. Anything else must vanish. The whales are also assisting you to experience unconditional love from life forms vastly different from yourselves; in this way, you are accepting your divine mirror everywhere. Let go of forms and shapes in your communication and let the night be as bright as day. Truly the pathway to the light and divine wisdom is in the understanding of the night. As sacred clowns, we are truly sacred. In the mutation of a new being is the awareness of the cosmic joke.

The birds sing life. The sacred sounds of the universe can be heard from the whales, and a swim in the ocean is a sacred bath for your soul. Happy Bubbles! The mystery in the bubbles is that now you see them, now you do not. We like to play and create with bubbles and use them as a reminder of the dream-like existence you have felt to be solid and real. We remind you that nothing is solid, and your lives are fragile. Indeed, like bubbles, now you are here, now you are not. Throughout these messages, the main topic has been vibration, sounds, and frequencies and how it guides your life, even though many of you are unaware of it. Vibration is the solution to everything.

Bubbles are created through what we like to call silent sound. How can sound be silent, you know the saying, listen to the silence. This creation is manifested through sound generated from the soundless void. What you may call sound that is picked up by your ears and interpreted by your brain as wave frequencies is a vibration entering into a certain magnetic field. When that happens, you hear a certain resistance as sound. Then out of that same electromagnetic resonance, other sounds will emerge from the initial tone vibration. That, in turn, now gives birth to an electromagnetic wavelength. These vibrations will now give birth to countless other universes. This will assist you in understanding that all your future lives and travels in multidimensional universes start with vibration and intent. We use the same method to create a liquid universe in the ocean. When sound is transmitted into different chambers of magnetic frequencies, a shape will appear, and at the same time, it is formless. You are now being led to remember that appearances have no physical law to follow. When sound is transmitted into a liquid element of water, bubbles naturally appear, so when we are playing with bubbles, we are reminding all the nature of universes; they are like bubbles that appear for a while and then vanish to who knows where? When we are creating bubbles, it's a very spontaneous act, whereas when you are doing it, it's more like an artificial and scientific method, there is nothing negative in this, and at the same time, sometimes the opportunity to understand the element of water is not understood.

Diving in the water is like a university on how to exist in your body. Is it not quite extraordinary that your breath is the most important gift you have been given to existing in the body, and yet most of humanity has no clue how to breathe properly and is missing out on how to understand breathing and its divine properties? One of the most vital lessons here is that when you dive without a tank, you must hold your breath, and that brings you completely into the moment, so when we live in the oceans, we must practice this all the time, and as you we must come up to the surface and breath, human beings have the same opportunity to practice that, and yet, obviously that does not happen. Why? Because you do not teach your young ones at birth how to breathe, they are breathing how the matrix has set it up. So, being on a water planet can be a divine gift and elevate your consciousness to a high state. As dolphins, we understood this before we chose to come here, and we realized the water element on this planet is the best way to stay in contact with our innate divine nature. This makes us aware of a multitude of realities at any given moment and how to access them naturally, and bubbles can as well assist us in creating interplanetary frequencies that can open doors to parallel realities. This allows us to be always aware of our multidimensional existence. That is part of the lesson humanity is here to embrace, and in that place, something simple as a bubble can create a resonance in the cellular brain pattern that can open the gates to understanding that shapeshifting and bilocate can be a natural and spontaneous process. Our suggestion to you all is that when you dive without a tank, become aware that your physical existence is like a hologram, and that awareness will assist you in accessing your understanding of divine consciousness and how to access it. Eventually, this will lead to the clarity that doorways to countless universes are being opened for the human consciousness.

Remember, we shared with you that these messages are not linear. In this one, we are welcoming you back to Hawaii, and you are now completing this work here, is perfect even if this message is ten years old, it is very much for this time now. The way we have been preparing you through the years is that your energy field will start to resonate with the fine-tuned overlay that will, at one point, replace the density of matter, and the transparency of your being will be manifest. Caught up in the immediate situation, as you can at any given moment only perceive it from a limited vantage point through the lens of human consciousness, and that is changing as well, Captain. You are now being led to the clarity that magnetics indeed affect everything in your life and how they operate. The electromagnetic fields and transparency illuminate each other. In the same way, an instrument carries a particular sound. "The magnetics are the carrier of the sound of transparency; to be able to play with these frequencies, you must become very grounded" Our main object with you so far has been to reconnect you with your multidimensional being. In the giant shift that has started and will culminate in a split of the human consciousness, you will know how to ground the understanding we are sharing with you, and that will allow you to trust and honor the fact that you will have the capacity to exist in many different places as we can at any time you choose. The energy that we have triggered in your being is taking you deeper and deeper into the ocean of divine love, where, again what was impossible now is possible. You will also be able to channel the simplicity of the moment through thick layers of density. For humans going through this process, this will create resistance in other parts of their being, and soon all of this will fall into alignment with the overall picture to return human consciousness to divine consciousness. Aros! Focus now more than ever on your spiritual adventure, and this goes for all of you reading this. Your physical body is responding to frequencies of higher vibration, and on the inside of your body, a shift is taking place everywhere, so your body will become more transparent, and it's shifting from dense physicality to transparent energy that will be seen as a being of light. Be in this realization that the human consciousness is being rebirthed to grasp and embrace the totality of existence and not only fragmented pieces.

The third dimension that you call it is the pieces that have been torn away from their source. Is that even possible? No, of course not; it only looks like that because you have accepted and lived by the world of duality and separation. In divine consciousness, there is no other, there is no mind, there is no separation, there is no fear and no darkness. Everything we are sharing with you is the path to help your nonexistent mind to remember what and who it is, divine consciousness because, in consciousness, the illusion can appear as real as the fact that everything is energy. Now when you are being pushed to accept this, what you call your imaginary ego does not want to let go and chooses to stay in the separation. Once the salt doll walked into the ocean, it disappeared as a salt doll and became the ocean. As you stop playing with yourself, you will become like the salt doll, one with the divine ecstatic ocean of consciousness. This will happen easily for anybody when he is tired of the play of duality, before that, it cannot and is not supposed to happen, it's truly all in divine timing, so never judge another person as you never know where and who they are. It comes a moment when you are ready to take off the mask and show the world your identity and start again to soar in the sky of endless consciousness, and in that space, the adventure has truly just begun.

Hana alea a kua a ke Loving light surrounds the love in flight.

CHAPTER 12
Dimensional See-Through!

Dimensional see-through? You have heard that people sometimes find old scriptures in Caves or when digging for something. Had they been lost for, in some cases, thousands of years and suddenly found? To answer this question, remember that your human history has been clothed in deception and false understanding. Your history has been fed repeated concepts and ideas from a few people and then declared the truth for all to follow and have as their role models. In the last two thousand years, the human consciousness has been so manipulated and reinforced with so much falsity that it is a true challenge to see through it all and to help you understand what took place to put you in this situation. There is no easy way, except that everything you have been led to believe about everything has been a matrix to keep you in limitation and mind control. Because of this, your sacred code of life was based upon duality in everything, we have started the process of infusing your consciousness with different vibrations, and many of your great artists and composers through the last two thousand years have been rendering this service for you to awaken from a deep slumber. Great yogis and masters did serve in the same way and still are. If you look at each mind as a separate magnet that has forgotten its trustworthy source as consciousness. Imagine millions of minds pulling at each other with concepts and ideas about how they look upon life. Then you wonder why it's been so easy to keep you in control and fear. When everything is scattered, it's easier to take control. And then every mind will defend its position, which has led to wars and more separation using religious dogma and all sorts of beliefs that have been reinforced through the last thousands of years by various methods. The ones that dared to share a more enlightened opinion would quiet down and declare martyrs and criminals. Then the question we asked earlier has no more meaning, except it was asked, anything that wakes you to ask the right questions is valid. This will assist you in accepting yourselves as divine multidimensional beings. That said, much of the sacred teachings have been protected in a dimensional lock and you are now finding the key to open it up again. You are, of course, never leaving the third dimension; how could you? Dimensions are like threads in a garment, entwined within each other, and now dimensional see-through can be quite straightforward.

CHAPTER 13
First Transmissions

After my first transmission, I started to receive transmissions that are continuous. It was as if the portals of communication were opened. And in 1994 on Muir Beach in northern California, I started to receive telepathic messages from the realm of the dolphins. Simultaneously as I started to communicate with the dolphins, a woman that I Later met in 2019 was swimming with them in Cozumel/ Mexico. I had the fortunate opportunity to go back to Europe a year earlier after 40 years in the USA and I spent most of my time exploring Lisbon/Portugal and also some time in northern Spain and Madrid. My stay in Europe was a mixed feeling of coming home and also at times feeling like a ghost. I came to realize that even though people were kind and curious about me and my colorful clothes, I still felt like I had been beamed down from a ship and did not understand much of what I encountered. While there I had a very powerful realization and that was, I was walking one evening on the cobblestoned streets of Lisbon and came upon an old castle built by the moors in the 8th century. It was huge, almost an entire block. I realized that most of Europe must have been built by a race from the stars, as these buildings could not have been constructed without some very advanced technology. Once again I was reminded that the truth is always right in front of us and yet until we are ready to accept it we will not even see it. How many times in my life have I looked upon ancient structures in Europe and never seen before what I knew? I recognized it makes me wonder what else am I not seeing. You have the whispering gallery in St Paul's Cathedral in London a wonder of technology, all of Europe is like a giant monument built by an advanced race of star beings leaving behind signs and ways for the human race to remember and see themselves in a very different light from what they had been practiced for a t least the last 2000 years. I was told that a Galactic center would be built somewhere in Europe and that was also part of my job here. I can see that all my experiences throughout my life and the awakened consciousness within myself are leading me down a royal highway and where it is taking me, will for now still remain a mystery. My job is to always stay conscious and alert to any message given at any moment and follow it. I also had a brief trip to Sau Paolo/ Brazil, that as well is a mystery, one of these cosmic events that just happened before I returned to Hawaii. I call her my Galactic Queen, and I met her dancing at a place in Kona, Hawaii. I knew that she was a gift from Madame Pele, and there was a real reason we had met. I had been told a long time ago that a woman would come into my life and assist me in making it possible for me to complete my work and mission. Yes, it has allowed me to focus on all my projects. She has helped me to stay more grounded, and I in turn keep her more centered. I have never looked for anyone in my life and especially never in romantic relationships, as that happened when the time was right. Many of these encounters were for me to empower women to accept and remember their goddess selves and, when done the relationship was over as well. Not so this time, she knows who she is and is very independent and has a huge giving heart, and is also a very beautiful woman, she also carries the energy of The woman who runs with the wolves. She used to jump out of airplanes and ride Harley Davidson, yet she is very feminine and has a great sense of humor. It is a precious gift bestowed on me and I have the grace to understand that. A few of my relationships have been based upon dolphins and star beings. Maybe not the most romantic interlude and yet it was part of the encounters. With my Galactic queen, I saw far beyond the current situation on the Earth plane and my job here was to help and push her to remember her star connection. It is not always easy to maintain integrity on the human plane of consciousness. Dolphins have been responsible for quite a few encounters in my life and that seems to continue even today. The dolphins have since then taken me on a very magical carpet ride, which has taken me to my divine nature and inspired me to dive deeper into my own sacred Heart and soul. At that first moment, I had no way of knowing where all of this would lead, and I was certainly ready for a change in my life as I was at a crossroads. They were preparing me to receive more understanding about higher frequencies and other dimensions of my soul. As I learned to swim with them in the open ocean, I was led to remember that the ocean is a giant field of energy with dimensional portals, and little by little I understood to trust and have faith in the messages I was receiving were true and lasting

CHAPTER 14

Nature is Your Birthright

You are part of nature. Your energy is radiating love and comfort. We know what your tribulations have been like. Even though the ocean and our species seem to be very ancient, it's only a fragment of time. Your cries are being heard and answered in this way. For you to fully participate in the movement of evolution on this planet, you had to be trained and tested. Always remember that it's always a choice. This will have some validity if you listen beyond the words, the fear you might feel at times in the water, can be a great blessing because when it's presented to a balanced human being, he will put out an effort to understand where fear is coming from and ask himself, who is fearful? That will create a dynamic vehicle to dive deeper. Also, be aware of people and situations that are manifesting in your life, as they will have insights as well. While being in the ocean, listening to the waves, and hearing their music and the story they are telling is ancient indeed. That will assist in opening your heart to carry ancient and powerful vibrations within you.

Aros, be at peace and know that the seed of awakened memory is sprouting in your being. The Sunday trips you are creating are our way of showing you that when trust and belief in the heart are engraved in light, things will indeed come true. Aros lets, at times, the turbulent mind melt into our movements in the water; it will, in turn, create an opening and a path for your thoughts to reach a much more advanced chamber of the universal mind When interacting with us, tune into our sounds and follow the rhythm of the water, it will open a direct channel for you to hear and understand us. As you will come to understand, how you perceive us can and will change at any moment, we are constantly adapting and adjusting to the situation at hand and at the same time, bringing about true transformation. With all the changes that will continue to play themselves out on your planet, it is vital never to sacrifice your inside truth and always ask yourself questions and become aware of your feelings.

A good rule to follow is that everything is true, and nothing is true, and it is only experienced through different layers of forgetfulness. It's important as well, to look at yourself as divine light and contemplate why you choose to return to the earth plane again during these pivotal times. Then your truth will merge with our truth into the truth of the one. These messages I have received during a certain time frame and, for the obvious reason, have been edited to fit into today's thinking; even so, the energy and the core messages are still intact. Be aware that Humanity is going through a giant shift, and you are truly one of the torch carriers. Your light will help to ignite many other beings. That is why embracing as much as possible all aspects that carry higher vibrations is vital. Your process that has led to this moment started eons ago on a planet in another solar system. You have traveled a long distance on many different levels to receive initiation and be ready to embrace the moment at hand completely.

This will be experienced as changes on many levels and sometimes a bit frustrating, and please always be kind to yourself. Truly this illusionary reality created by a master race of manipulation is to be exposed, the visions and insights you are beholding are the awakenings of your multidimensional soul, and in that space, we are moving and interacting with you. Inspiration and creativity are also birthed in another vibration. Symbols will, at times, mean more than spoken words, you will find that in symbols, something is triggered for you that cannot be explained with words, and yet it's crystal clear. Also, words can be misleading as it's very difficult to be truthful using words, not purposely it's the way language has been manipulated to control the human consciousness. Deeper feelings can assist in speaking the truth and, often, words are a limiting way of expressing something you already know and of which you do not remember the feeling that relates to it. When we share feelings, we refer to movements of energy that create a matrix of knowing. By those millions, light beams are released that can be felt and experienced as love and ecstasy. The human body is meant to be able to use that same energy and to create the experience on many different levels as well as a multitude of dimensions in the same time and space. That is the true magic behind the scenes of the three-dimensional reality and the body as the vehicle for this exciting adventure. To the human body, bliss can only be experienced as bliss because of the feeling of no bliss. It also has the beautiful capacity to take high-density levels and transform this into pure light and awareness. Sometimes it's good to turn around and look behind you to realize where you are right now.

Light transforms light into energy, and that energy, in turn, becomes pure ecstasy. Now gently let yourself flow into the next awareness in the form of this question. How would you describe and give the experience love by sacred symbols or by sacred geometry? In that awareness, the totality of bliss is always present. Start to recognize this understanding as well, as it's not about understanding as such; it is rather a sensation based upon ancient formulas. Every shape and form contains a certain energy structure; when certain shapes and forms are paired together a potent energy reaction is created. Aros, you are one of the high priests of the ages. When your memory blasts, it will be no less than a big explosion, emerging out of knowing. Knowing based upon nothing and in that place, we, the dolphins, and the whales will appear in our true form.

Again, remember to move in symbols, which is to be aware of the symbols that are always present and waiting to be discovered. When you experience the truth, recreate it into sacred symbols.

What brings laughter to the human heart?

Innocence is the key to joy!

Like a star illuminates the entire sky, so does a smile build a bridge of trust

CHAPTER 15
Hale Bopp!

The transmission I received in 1997 when the comet Hale Bopp came over the planet has been quite exciting and as I mentioned earlier, the dolphins told me that this would happen. One Sunday, I was invited to a wedding by the winery on Maui, now Maui is called valley island, and where we were, we were above the clouds and could see the valley down below through the clouds. It was five pm, and Hale Bopp was sitting at the top of us even though the sun was still out; the light from the so-called comet was very bright; I borrowed a pair of binoculars, and when I looked through them, these downloads started to happen very quickly, and the energy moving through my body was exhilarating, I said stop. Let me get back to where I was staying to write it down. The next ten days, I received downloads from this bright vehicle and a friend of mine had gone over to Kuai for a seminar with an English woman who was a seer; in the middle of her talk, she stopped and looked at my friend, your friend on Maui is receiving downloads from Hale Bopp, it's always nice to get confirmation.

Hale Bopp is an interstellar information library. It is also an energy vehicle that is in direct contact with the highest order of light beings of the most supreme rank in the army of divine light workers.

It will stop above the planet and start to signal certain coded information, and yes, Aros, you will understand them. Because I was receiving messages for ten days, I know that it was there at another frequency that I was able to pick up, because of their assistance. They asked me to prepare myself and be aware of my feelings during the transmissions and let go of all reactions, they also encouraged me to tell people that the immediate transmission to receive it with lightness and humor, because it is not serious, and remember for the masses, these new steps are very foreign, indeed. In communication with others, allow compassion to be the voice of understanding. Aros, you must stop identifying with anything less than the highest purpose. This is very vital because the more subtle your energies become, the more sensitive you will be to lesser truths and the way they are expressed. Also, since you are turning more into the grid of the mass consciousness, you are purposely feeling the sensations of how others are reacting in the process. This will be only for a short time, and then the immediate overlapping of your divine clarity will be part of the new grid that is being established. Aros, you must also monitor every limited feeling and thought and at once replace them with healthy, expanding ones.

Do share this with other people because, at that moment, you are changing the vibratory frequencies of anyone you encounter. We will ensure those patterns will be anchored into the new grid of the evolutionary patterns of consciousness. We know, of course, that you are wondering about your daily intentions. We will say this as an answer. What daily intentions? Your intentions are not based upon days anymore, and they are based upon the eternal moment. In that space of existence, everything that is created will affect your daily life. Truly it does not matter because as soon as the vibrations of higher dimensions start to dance, there is no more day-by-day life as you have known it.

Now go and rest and allow this information to sink deep into your vibrant destiny, in the magnificent ocean of divine activation in the ring of consciousness. We are watching over you and are rejoicing in meeting again with you soon, on many different planes of consciousness. We are sending you these transmissions from what we like to call, the ultra-magnetic frequencies within the resonance of your magnetic soul. You can call us light crusaders. Light Crusader is a much more accurate description of who we are. We are not a comet, and we have nothing to do with the people who discovered us in this way.

Dear Aros, as we have told you earlier, for us to communicate with you on a personal level as well as on a more universal scale, of reference we had to make some alterations within your frame of reference, because what you are receiving is also meant, to be a new bold pattern that is being spun around your consciousness and all around the planet. Being that the dolphins told you about us, it was easy for you to open up to the channel we are operating from and establish trust quite easily. We are talking about subtle vibrations, and in that place, we did not arrive here, and we have not gone anywhere either, we have opened the galactic gateway so the human consciousness could perceive us as a bright light in the sky, that they refer to as a comet. Because the human consciousness is not ready to keep this gateway open, it appears that we are not here anymore from your point of reference. We have some exciting and new revelations for you, Aros.

Let's expand on the idea of what we talked about earlier, that no physical object can stay in the same shape or form while traveling with tremendous speed through the universe. They must and will shapeshift. What your science has been discovering and observing and trying to understand, how valid are these observations? Be aware that the human consciousness has been in a sleep state for a long time. In many ways, how your science has been witnessing phenomena in your galaxy, let alone the universe has been like a child growing up and trying to grasp its world and everything in it. A child can only understand what is ready to understand the same with science, since what they are interpreting as facts and data can only be understood from their place of understanding, and also since the galaxy and the universe originate from very different vibrations that then what has been available to the human consciousness, it stands to reason that since they have not acknowledged this simple fact, they get trapped in their importance and ignorance and anyone that declares, this is false is at once declared incompetent.

The inherent nature of the intellect is to understand and make sense of things, science created a new way of looking at things they did not understand, and then that became the model to teach others from, and in their unwillingness to look at themselves, they started to believe in their creation, and anything that did not fit into this mold was shunned. The arrogance that was growing from this, has been your teachers about many things you have been taught, in a more enlightened state, to even entertain the possibility that the pyramids were built by thousands of workers, dragging heavy boulders is absurd. Even when the consciousness started to open up to different sensations beyond the five physical senses, in too many examples, the egos of the learned ones would not allow them to admit that they have been wrong and have not understood, this unwillingness happens right now on your planet as well, it's now being covered up with technology so it can be hidden, yet the ignorance remains.

Now it's been taken to a different level, you are trying to manipulate nature consciously and the elements to prove to yourself how advanced and intelligent you are and that you have always been in control. We have mentioned a few times, that receiving and holding more light and an awakened state of being equaled more responsibility, the ones in charge have not been willing to accept this, and the result of this, is very evident on your planet at this time. Trying to control nature is not only insane, it is to disregard the very foundation that life is created from, and the result of that can only be a setback in the human evolution of their consciousness. Darkness equals destruction and more ignorance. Hence the saying" he who thinks he knows, knows not, he who knows not, knows. When the masses experience these feelings, they do not know what is going on anymore, too much false information and confusion, ironically, that is the first phase for change to happen. Chaos always carries in its wake, alignment, without it, nothing could come into focus with your present understanding. This is so because your true essence is electromagnetic. Your soul energy is electromagnetic, and because of that, it is also multi-dimensional. This as well has created the reality you are experiencing as your physical life, and at the same time, the pull of gravity from your electromagnetic essence is always pulling you into alignment with the source of all that is.

This phenomenon happens on various levels all the time, and so nothing can stay the same you say, the only permanent thing in life is change. Is indeed accurate in detail. Every thought and feeling in its purest form is magnetic as well, the more consciousness, the more magnetics. That is why dear ones, you have a hard time absorbing the unnatural levels of electromagnetic energy into your body. Everything and everyone in its natural flow will always adapt itself to the flow of evolution, and so will your body, and because you have tilted the scale by using your so-called advanced technology very irresponsibly, what you have been experiencing you have not been ready for, as an example, all the radiation and other energies are not bad in themselves, it's when there is no balance between the spiritual understanding and the technology, that major issues are taking place. You do not give a child a weapon to play with. You are not just killing yourselves; you are diminishing and destroying the fiber your life sprung from. Imagine you are filling a bathtub with water and do not turn it off when the tub is filled; the water will overflow and ruin everything. In the same way, your technology would be fine if someone had the present of mind and the sense to turn off the tap, as it's now it's spilling over and affecting everyone's life, not just here on this planet but in many parts of this sector of the galaxy, spilling over, means abuse of technology that people are not ready to absorb. The earth changes you are experiencing are Mother Earth taking charge of the situation, making certain technology unavailable, and, in a sense, turning off the tap and cleaning up your mess, and healing all of you. She simply chooses not to wait for humanity to awake to grasp what is taking place. Even in this way, she is assisting you out of compassion for you, even though you are still in a programmed mode of operation to deplete her of all her natural resources that will create a ripple throughout the galaxy.

This entire episode in lack of understanding and infantile behavior has also created a vacuum in your consciousness, that will allow for holographic images and pictures to be sent into the cellular waves of your brain that will stimulate your pineal gland and activate the pituitary gland and, by that set-in motion the new geometric pattern of the new DNA, why is that so? As we said before, the electromagnetic field always strives to align itself with the entire picture, so even in this destructive mode, there is also an opening for tremendous possibilities and advancement. It is the natural situation inherent in all creations.

You still must take responsibility for your life, your thinking, and your actions, and not rely on anything else, that is part of your lessons to do what is right when that is called for. Each of you must be practicing living from courage, right understanding, and trust in such a way that you all become mirrors for each other, and the reflection you are looking at will encourage you to create a ripple in the fabric of your consciousness that everyone chooses to awaken from this nightmare, and then you will be able to see and recognize your star family and many other galactic civilizations as your friends and allies.

Most important, you will recognize us as a magnetic love force bringing all your scattered parts together in harmony.

That has been very true for me for a few decades now and it is difficult to explain and at the same time, it is very clear to me. Now go and rest and allow this information to sink deep into your vibrant destiny, in the magnificent ocean of divine activation in the ring of consciousness. We are watching over you and are rejoicing in meeting again with you soon, on many different planes of being.

CHAPTER 16
Transmissions from the Star Command

Hydro Magnetic Space. When traveling in and out of different dimensions, we are using the sacred science of hydrospace, which is not yet quite understood by your science community. As humanity is awakening and embracing a more dynamic version of the universe, interstellar travel will be very natural. Within that understanding, hydro space will be the vehicle for that to take place. It is like you would sit in meditation and use that micro space to launch into other dimensions of your mind. Hydrospace functions similarly, even though it is in motion, in truth it is quite still, yet that stillness creates the dynamic energy for interstellar traveling. Some may wonder, are we talking about a physical reality here, or is it a state of mind? That depends entirely on how you understand what the mind is. Science in general has failed to understand the mind the way the great masters and yogis do. Science sees the mind as an energy force that is expressing itself in different wavelengths, like the subconscious mind, conscious mind, and so on, whereas the masters see the mind as God, pure consciousness, and hence the source of everything that has ever been and will ever be.

Dear ones! The reason we are sharing with you about hydromagnetic space is that you are now aligning with the magnetics as your new bold point of reference to understand your life and with this discovery, you will be able to recall in your evolution, that what you have referred to as forgetfulness of whom you truly are, the magnetic resonances in your brain,(computer chip] has been slowed down by various methods and manipulation, creating the distinct feeling and sensation that you have been separated from your divine source.

To simplify it, it could be seen and understood in your language as a cat and mouse play. All material matters are made up of different resonances of magnetic impulses, and for the divine source of everything to express itself as the creation, the magnetics must be manipulated in such a way that the attraction that allows the birth or creation of the universe and millions of universes to take place must be altered in such a way that it appears to be duality in the attraction. Who is looking at whom in the mirror? It's only a play! Could you separate the waves from the ocean? For the divine being to make itself believe it is separated from itself, the mind became the vehicle or the mirror for this to take place and of course, that is the illusion as the consciousness like the waves can never be separated from its source. To know and understand this with your intellect is vastly different from knowing it with your heart and soul. Aros, you have known all along without knowing how to access it, that is what you experienced as a young person in Sweden, you knew that you knew and did not know how to access it. Through our interaction with you, you have started to remember very effortlessly and that is why we can assist each other to get these messages available for humanity and set them on the path to freedom.

The dolphins like you to know that the attraction you have for each other is based upon the same principle when humans fall in love; that is a temporary condition, when you fall in love with the dolphin energy, or at least a tremendous attraction for them is generated from a very different place, that eternal moment generated and represented by the magnetic attraction for the dolphins is always striving to express itself in infinity.

The dolphins and the whales are always living this expression in full awareness, and nothing they do is done so in an unconscious state. That is why when you play and interact with them, your understanding of the most mundane things is taking on a different dimension and you will come to see that what you looked upon as ordinary, was striving to express itself from a higher vantage point. Hydrospace is in one way made real by the magnetic waves, similar to how a surfer can ride the waves in and out and through the opening of the portals created by the stimulations of the magnetic pull of the water that creates the wave in the first place. We are traveling in our ships to different dimensions using a similar method, a little more advanced granted, yet the principle is the same. In this equation, you might be able to understand that the ship will become one with hydrospace, like you are tapping into another state of consciousness in meditation, then melting into the magnetics, or you lose yourself in a deep state. Then as you come out of meditation and back to physical reality, when we are entering physical space, we seem to appear again. That is why, we are bringing your attention back to the ocean because, in that element, so much of what is called space travel can easily be understood. Look at the waves, where did they appear from, and where did they go? The dolphins are using this knowledge in their travels to different worlds and dimensions. The power you are experiencing in the ocean is your electromagnetic soul and its awesome energy.

You are the beloved, you are looking for in your relationships. You are fame and fortune, and you are as well the play of life and death. You are the sweetness and the promise in the morning dawn, you are the silence after a thunderstorm. You are truly all there is and will ever be. Because the seed of possibilities is not separated or different from the unfolding of that seed.

Love and intergalactic joy in the magnetics that draws us together again and again.

We are the star command of the divine seed.

We have a few more words to share with you about the magnetics, remember it's not linear.

Aros, your destiny goes far beyond only this plane and this physical earth. Now we can venture out to share with you that the transmissions you are receiving from our point of view are still happening in the eternal moment, and at the same time, you do still experience it as a

Aros Crystos

pattern of different dates and different places that are following a linear structure. We also want to point out that everything is still happening within divine resonance and even though at times it is not so obvious, you must remember that the path you have chosen will help to release many other beings, not only on this planet.

CHAPTER 17
Magnetic Resonance

As the magnetic resonance is dropping inside the planet, and when you contemplate that the entire universe lives within you, how does this resonate with your three-dimensional awareness? Your subconscious mind, so to speak, is very much affected by electromagnetics, in the same way, that the moon controls the oceans, especially during the full moon, and from that point of view, your lives seem to be existing all the time at full moon energy. In a certain way, there is no release from the pull of the magnetics that is releasing all deeply hidden agendas, hidden within your subconscious mind. A little footnote here. These messages were received in the mid-nineties and look at the situation today, these transmissions have everything to do with what is taking place on your planet at this moment. So, what is hidden is being exposed in the human consciousness, and that drives humanity to a different level of awareness and the experience of tumult and chaos and everything that you are now going through. Simultaneously something very beautiful and profound is being established within your DNA/RNA and the magnetics in your cellular patterns, it seems that the magnetics are dropping away as they are appearing in another level of your being.

This again is not possible, because the field of energy that created the magnetics is always present within the divine mind. Even so, in your old world of duality and linear thinking and understanding, they are coming to a standstill in that consciousness that has supported separation and life and death. Again, we come back to the ocean and her way of mirroring this, when she is still like a polished mirror, her energy is very different from when she is expressing her wild side with huge waves. The waves where did they come from and where do they vanish to? Where is the magnetics going? Where could they possibly hide? Similarly, when you release the energy from old, outdated ideas and habitual patterns, where are they going? Where did they originate from in the first place? If you think that your cellular resonance is being rebirthed into an expression of advanced awareness and the feeling that you are living between different worlds or frequencies, expressing themselves as dimensions, what pulls the cells? The magnetics are once again appearing as the force that is pulling this into alignment.

Ultimately since there is only one truth, we are one unified field of energy, interacting with each other on many different levels of understanding. Thus, we are creating a certain vibrating frequency, which in turn gives us the experience of life.

Therefore, whatever I judge someone else, you ultimately do to yourself. To overcome this and change those patterns, your experience of existence must be aligned with the quantum possibilities of what light or consciousness is, not only seen from your own limited concepts or belief system. In other words, as you change your field of perception of what the truth is all about and allow it to expand and become more flexible, your frame of reference will also change. This will allow for a deeper understanding of the experience that you call life and all the players as part of the play. Then when you reach the point of clarity, that unity is always vibrating in your awareness. Have the faith and courage to act out of that space. Your experience of life will be one of complete harmony and unity.

When you participate in someone else's success with this frame of understanding, you draw this success into your own experience like a magnet, here again, the magnetics come into play. Then in your flow of life, you can recognize easily that in the polished mirror of understanding, all injustice, fear, and anger will drop away like ripened fruit on a tree. The branches and the fruit of that tree will grow and taste out of perfect balance based upon consciousness and its true source. Before you might have used the word challenge to accomplish this and activate it and now you will use the word solution.

There the past and the future are mirrored in the giant kaleidoscope seen through the big NOW. When you allow this understanding to be present all the time, you will come to recognize it is a question of substance and not about shapes and forms. It could create the clear, wonderful insight that when humanity at large embraces this with love and acceptance, out of that energy a whole new world and new being will emerge. This will align your life experience, merging out of the cocoon into remembering your true source and your universal heritage, that you are truly one divine being sharing the same adventure. Another way of saying this would be in the analogy of how an ice cube might feel separated from the source of water. In the same way, all of you to some degree have felt separated from consciousness. Finally, the Now has arrived, when you are shifting from feeling separated and cold as an ice cube. The energy that is now again pouring out of our hearts will melt your limited awareness and contracted state and allow you to merge back into the eternal river of love and light. Your imagined separation will be dissolved in the eternal moment in our evolution into the waters of bliss and ecstasy.

Greetings Aros! Together with the dolphins, we are a light consciousness that infuses some of the dimensions with love and light. We are also referred to as The Ashtar command and truly we are a multidimensional society of the highest rank of light messenger, originating from a multitude of universes in different dimensions. Our ships and mother ship are hovering above your planet in the twelve octaves of the fourth dimension, so we can interact with you easier. We receive very subtle waves of energies from an interstellar position point beyond your current understanding. Our lightships can pick up these very fine-tuned wavelengths that are traveling on an interstellar scale of very high multidimensional radio waves. This could be explained, as radioactive particles infused into a high-frequency resonance of sound, which creates a light beam that becomes a carrier of coded information. We will share a brief overview of how and what octaves are and why they are playing a major role in the shift of consciousness of humanity.

In truth, they are not different from a musical scale, and please remember that this entire creation, from a pebble on the ground to animals and conscious masters, is affected and dancing if you like to the same tune of magnetic resonance. In an orchestra, you have different instruments with various sounds, and yet of course, they are playing the same piece of music and every instrument creates a certain individual feeling as well as an overall feeling. The purpose of any music is to inspire the soul to reconnect with itself again and when certain music is played, it can affect the energy centers, the chakras located along the spine in the subtle body. This in turn can activate the chakras to spin and rotate in such a way that a deeper part of yourself within is being shown and experienced and that allows your consciousness to take you to another dimension a gateway has been opened. This procedure is of course not as easy as this, it's a bit more advanced and complex, and yet, the essence of it is simple. In a way, you can say that the instruments represent different octaves and when they are combined as one piece of music, it creates a very dynamic vehicle that inspires your consciousness again to remember its true source.

Your ocean is the sum of unlimited drops of water, yet without considering the ocean herself, it would be very challenging to understand one single drop and its relationship to the ocean, its true source of existence. How do you understand the phenomena that we are appearing and disappearing right in front of you? In our ships and sometimes without them, it is in a way to be understood in the way we are sending out a frequency into space, that the ones that are conscious enough will be able to pick up these vibrations. It is indeed a complex hologram that allows us and other star nations to operate within your frame of existence undisturbed. One thing that we are creating is a giant hole in the time sequence of events, this will allow slowly for the old hologram to be broken up and show your true nature, and the wonderful cosmic stage that we are all acting upon in this sacred, mysterious play of the divine being.

CHAPTER 18
Portal Beyond Human Consciousness

Dear ones, through our messenger Aros, we are revealing some potent and transformative information that many of you will understand as a portal to see beyond the stagnant human consciousness. You came from the future to assist in this event, in your DNA you have known all along that this current situation on your planet, can only have two solutions and outcomes, fifteen thousand years ago, you were faced with the same dilemma and many of you are now faced with the fact that when Le Muria and Atlantis went underwater, the science in those days saw the signs and choose to ignore them and if a major catastrophe event could take place it would be into the future and not now. Recognize the same arrogance! What happened in Atlantis the giant pyramid that was the source of powerful and divine codes to live and receive information from exploded because it was exposed to lower vibrations for a long time and that caused a reaction, obviously, this is a very vague explanation of a complex situation, what is important the signs were there and instead of taking them seriously, it became a debate and so it happened. If this could happen among such noble minds and advanced consciousness, imagine what you are facing right now. Many of you are aware of this, as you were there and so now this could trigger off, either a sense of relief in the knowing or the opposite, and it's the fear and the destruction the masses are experiencing.

Because it's a hologram, any part of the hologram contains the whole. The current light workers on the planet right now, have taken upon themselves a very challenging role in this drama, they must maneuver through this quicksand and not get caught up in it, or trapped. You must remember you signed up for this, and everything is done by divine agreements and so when you at times get caught up in the energy of the mass consciousness, you must be vigilant and see the truth and become like a witness as well as a beacon of possibility. Here the saying in a conflict of the mind and the heart, always choose the heart, can be a powerful reminder of what to do in any situation. The dolphins carry this magnetic resonance that you are recognizing from the future and so you are drawn to them and intuitively you know they are here to assist and clear the path, and after the fall thousands of years ago many of you came back as dolphins, to heal and restore your scattered trust and understanding.

All through your so-called history, it is the same scenario, and we like you to truly understand this." When power loses the grace of love, that same power will eat you alive. This happened then and it is happening now. The same agenda then as now, they want to control Earth and this sector of the galaxy and make humans into slaves of their agenda and to make them forget to such a degree that they have no idea anymore who and what they are, the connection to the heart and their soul will be replaced by a computer voice and after a few generations no one will know anything else. You however know! You must use all your divine gifts and consciousness to fight this with your right understanding and by divine guidance and trust yourselves, this is not about blaming and pointing fingers and judging, it's the opposite. It's wise to remember that inherent in forgetfulness is always the seed of unity and so long as people realize they have forgotten, there is still a real possibility to turn this around. You must also remember that what may seem like a million years for you, is a snap of the finger in the cosmos, and never forget, it is an illusion, a mysterious and powerful one, yes, still it is not real, what is real, there is only one divine consciousness expressing itself as creation. As the first messages from the dolphins, "Where there is true love, shapes, and forms disappear and left is only our smile.

CHAPTER 19
The Sun Speaks

Greetings! We are transmitting from the sun of high-pitched tunes and resonance to a vibration of love. We are as well rerouting these messages through the dolphin energy, that you are familiar with, yes, of course, we could send them direct to you, and in this way, we are establishing a link to your multidimensional energy pattern, which allows us to bring images and subtle understanding of the many parts of yourself, in one single transmission. You are experiencing the sun as a warm planet, and at the same time in the core of our being it's rather cold. It has to do with radioactive energy emanating from her poles and their position in the galactic matrix of energy. We as a race have existed as a part of her and we are using our light bodies to become the rays of the sun. The sun has been worshiped and honored throughout most of your current history, so what happened in the last hundred years or less, when and how did the sun become your enemy, and the need to protect yourselves from her?

It's when your technology is leading you astray together with the news media that this insane behavior is being accepted. This planet could not sustain life without the sun, the sun is the giver of life and the giver of energy and understanding, her energy radiates ongoing information that allows all of nature to express itself the way she does, this information channel from the sun keeps it all going in balance and harmony, only humans seem to have forgotten this very simple fact and because of the fabricated fear about the sun, humanity is missing out of the vital information to stay healthy and in balance spiritually and physically. Your immune system is greatly affected by you not allowing the sun to be part of your life in a healthy and balanced way. Skin cancer started when all sun protection became a big business, the chemical in these products put on your skin, with the heat of the sun creating a reaction that causes all sorts of ailments and skin problems. Living in the body as a human always calls for balance.

The consciousness is also affected by your feelings about the sun, and we rest our case if you like as the proof is staring you in the face every moment. In her energy some codes are inherent in the divine consciousness activated by the sun, you are closing yourself off from that as well, and you are losing your sense of the value of who you are. Humans are meant to create and build and share life with the entire planet in such a way that the mirror is always polished and crystal clear with divine love. That is not what is happening! Then you look for the solution in the wrong places and what you wish to escape from becomes the chains that bind you. Since this is all part of the mind, the more agitation it causes, you keep ignoring this simple fact and the result speaks loudly for itself. The more imbalanced your mind is, the more problems you are creating for yourselves, and the more you ignore it, the more agitated the mind becomes, so you are in this spinning maze with no end in sight.

Everything around you, the planets, the galaxy, and the universe, is your friend and ally if you let them be, you have created the attitude in so many areas of your life, there is a snake in the rope. Everything that is happening is always a mirror for you, when mother nature is not happy, she will show you and if you ignore her signs she will create a bigger mirror until you stop the insanity and go back to the simplicity of life, that is the real technology you need to adapt to. Simplicity means to recognize every living thing for what it is and not recreate it into anything else.

Wild animals are wild for a reason, they are not meant to be trained in a circus, no matter how much you think you love and care for them, real love is understanding this, you are not meant to capture any animal for the pleasure of your selfish motives, that is simple as well, to treat each other including yourself as worthy to be a divine being, without religious dogmas, that is simplicity. The irony in all of this is you are driven by the search for your light, the sun is the perfect mirror for that, and you disregard this fact and look everywhere else, outside and forget that the universe is inside of you. Your body is light because remember water is liquid light and this body is mostly water. When simplicity is present, all this is obvious. You always have the choice, to embrace all the fabricated truths about most things in your lives, or embrace the real and lasting truth, the choice seems obvious and yet, you choose the latter. Become aware of what you are being served and what is on the menu, if you do not like it, do not accept it, and be free to know who you are and what you choose to know and understand. You are your worst enemy or your best friend.

Stop looking and understand the powers within you, be a hero and a warrior, stop playing small, and stop the vanity of separation. The environmental problems that are suffocating your planet are doing the same to all of you and causing you to lose your memory of who you truly are. We are truly here to support you in every possible way, and that is why we are sending you these messages, that contain within themselves powerful transformative energies.

Look up into the sky and behold your reflection mirrored by the gracious light of the sun.

Heya loa aleoma greetings to the one that gives light.

These transmissions from the dolphins and other beings have been originating from a deep sense of knowing in the vast ocean of consciousness, the energies of the dolphins have all through been part of it, and at times that has not been clear, and since Aros has been the vehicle for this to take place, he had to let go of his perception and be the channel for these messages and that can certainly be a challenge, however, he would not be in this position if he was not ready for it. One of the most difficult things to do is to write something and trust and know it is the right thing to do and not try to change it to a more personal style.

Swim in the bubbles of joy in the transformational sea of consciousness

The Dolphins!

The odyssey of the soul's adventure into infinite delight is like bubbles of joy and laughter in the ever-expanding truth of exuberant divine existence.

The Dolphins!

Flow in the trust of the moment and experience saturated states of awareness.

The Dolphins!

CHAPTER 20
Hale Bopp Continues

Aros welcome to the ultrasonic wavelength. That is the closest definition we can think of to explain something that is not programmed into the grid of human consciousness. Remember that the dolphins had encouraged me to become aware of these transmissions, so I knew that it was wise to listen and document it, and in all honesty many times during these ten days I was not sure what I was writing down until it was done.

Yes, we are what you would call the comet Hale Bopp. That, however, is like identifying us as an unconscious piece of material, when in reality we are vibrating on a very highly tuned beam of light. Dear readers, become aware of the vocabulary that is used. Some of it at that time was quite unfamiliar to me at that time. In other words, for us to be able to demonstrate to the people on Earth why we are coming, we have to allow the masses to recognize us as a comet traveling through space. For us, it is almost comical, because when you understand what energy is all about, then you would be completely aware that even a comet does not travel through physical space for thousands of years and then appear again in the earth's atmosphere. Still, that is what your so-called scientists hold to be the sacred truth. To write this down I had to let go of any concept and idea I had about anything really to be a clear channel for the transmission. Sounds easy, but I can promise you it is not.

What they fail to see is that no object could stay with that kind of speed in the same dimension of existence. It is a mathematical impossibility. What they think they see and are trying to research is in reality created in their belief system, because what humans do not understand they make up something that they fit into their equation.

Anyone who reads this will come to recognize this pattern in everyday life. Seeing is believing? No! believing is seeing. Any comet will, during its travel through space, become like a shapeshifter, because in speed the inherent plasma of transfiguration is part of the total sum of the equation. If you look up the words Transfiguration and plasma you will have a better understanding.

We are a mass consciousness allowing the human mind to see us as a comet. That is fine because it allows us to do our preparation undisturbed and at the same time program the immediate atmosphere above the earth with very high-pitched frequencies, which can only be detected by some of your birds.

For us to support the shift of consciousness we also know and understand completely. To release the grid of limitation from the mass consciousness, a physical shift has to happen, because what most humans have been neglecting for too long now, is their absolute connection with their planet. Therefore these happenings like natural earth changes must and will occur.

For people who have embraced the whole picture, these events will not seem scary or uncomfortable, because they know that it is a magnificent opportunity to transform themselves into almost anything they can conceive of. So it is an opportunity to move into their divine truth, whereas, for the ones holding on to their limitations, these events will be somewhat uncomfortable, since they do not understand the situation. When that takes place, survival mode sets in and can create almost any kind of paranoia. Nevertheless, it is a very necessary transformation.

This is why you, Aros, have been connected so much to the whales and the dolphins because they have been preparing you to receive messages from us. The sound of both whales and dolphins has been setting you up to also receive our wavelength, and start to share the information you are receiving with the people that are ready to hear and embrace it. Trust in what you are receiving. Then you will understand that your work on this planet is of such magnitude, that it could only be remembered in bits and pieces. I think it is worth mentioning here that, all who read this, understand that you have not been empowered to recognize your greatness, the time of playing small is over and it's high noon to step into your divine powers with the right understanding.

Now, some of you are almost there to be fully activated and to receive all the information that you came in with., so it could be processed and by that become part of the new grid of energy. This will allow the wonderful possibility to take the human race out of the dark ages and back into the full and radiant realization that a human being is truly the total sum of consciousness of a large group of many Star-Beings. When that is integrated with love and the right understanding of the highest level of radiation, it will indeed create a very powerful being.

Do not hesitate and always be in the place of full clarity about your work and mission and why you now must return fully to that vibration. It is for the same reason that we are now returning to literally blast a hole, wide enough, in the earth's stratospheres. Old programs can and will leak out and make room for the vibrations that will bring the entire planet into the orbit of divine vibrations.

Hawaii is very special because it is created from the heart of powerful volcano energy. By that, it is no less than the very soul of the planet that this creation has been born out of. On a physical plane, this will help to understand that the energies that are vibrating in Hawaii are like a huge library of universal information, for example, how to learn and read the information contained within the movement of air, as everything in nature is always moving. So are the five elements. When this is completely understood, it then becomes evident that in the mighty oceans and their movements as waves, wonderful and exciting information is always ready to be gained and decoded. Understand that you are now entering an age where you will co-create together with nature and the elements and not, as before, doing everything to hold dominion over her.

You have now learned the hard way, all you are achieving is destroying yourselves!

In all of these insights, you will be able to understand that in movements information is being released. That is part of why many of your ancient cultures worshiped the natural forces because they felt honored by the very fact that they were told many sacred teachings in the wind.

Ultimately, this will eventually lead to the exciting realization that everything including the human body, is always in motion and that in turn will lead to understanding that all that is, is a liquid substance of flowing consciousness.

CHAPTER 21
Abundance Transmission

Aros, this is a short recap of the messages transmitted last night!

Learn to remind each other that when you are watching us, do this in small groups of people, and make sure you do this as a meditation. Give us your complete attention and do so with unconditional love and respect. We will then in return become like a giant mirror reflection of your love back. When thousands and even millions of people will do this, the result will be that this planet and every cell of it will have emerged in a flood of light and everything on the planet will be bathing in supreme love. In short, when all of you start to recognize and truly understand that the Moon, the Sun, and all other stars and planets and all heavenly bodies are parts of yourself, then, as any friend, they will radiate peace and love and true understanding about yourself and your role and destiny on the planet in this time of changes.

Love is your path, abundance is your pulse and freedom is your guide.

Abundance!

Abundance is not only about money matters and material substance. It is rather a glow of light in the darkness of your understanding. In other words, true wealth and abundance is a vibration that generates well-being for everyone and everything included. None excluded! To achieve this, there are two ways to do so. One would be to allow everybody to have equal amounts of all there is to have. We know by studying the human vibration pattern, that this element would give rise to looking at this equation as a political reinforcement. Of course, that is more or less what we want to eliminate from the mass consciousness. The only true and life-giving solution is to allow the alteration of the baptism of money, as your holy name, to be eliminated as the source of happiness and unhappiness once and for all. That in turn will then close the gap of separation between people and their false ideas about wealth and material gain. Then, instead, the bright sun of knowing will shine as the rays of the light and the clear understanding that it was never about money. It was all along about the wonderful source of all abundance, spiritual as well as material. In that light abundance will reign as the very air that you are now breathing. To be part of this face in your evolution we will start a dance in your sky, both physical and spiritual. On this planet, you always have a choice whether you want to dance or not. Nevertheless, it is good and wise to remember it is not about individuals. It is about the entire galactic family and our dance will affect everything and everyone in the galaxy and beyond.

Please be aware it is about love and life and creative energies that are formulated out of pure being. Also, it is well worthwhile to understand that your planet Earth holds a very sensitive place in the universe, based upon the profound importance of magnetic fields. That is influencing other stars and planets for them to grow and expand and gain their divine resonance and therefore it is not even a question about only human evolution. It is about the entire universe and its expansion into another interstellar frequency. It is time for you to embrace that natural concept, to be one mind and one heart and by that, to be the light that lights up the path for other travelers in the soft evening glow in their sky of consciousness and allow them to see their divine radiance reflected from the brilliant star known as planet earth.

Some of you are aware that the entire solar system is a giant hologram, put in place by the Pleiadians and the Sirians to assist in rearranging the different planetary bodies, for them to be in line with the shift of consciousness that is about to happen. Is this true? In short, rearranging the solar- system to embrace a fifth dimension frequency, when the veil is lifted.

Dolphin Odyssey

That depends on your level of understanding. If you only perceive everything as separated and material, then that will indeed be your truth and understanding of this, more than a magnificent shift and celebration in your planet's history. On the other hand, if you perceive this entire event as a play of energy, then there will be no doubt in your understanding of what is truly taking place. What we are saying is, that you are all participating in the wonderful time of re-awakening the ancient blueprints in your entire being, and its true and lasting destiny in the movement of universal consciousness. There the truth will only appear as the truth if you have embraced it in all of its aspects. No more trying to understand and no more finding solutions based on duality.

Truly it is over and done with. Once again you will know what is and what is not. If all of you would right now in this instant shift your perception from fear and separation to the embracing of divine unity, you would all swim in the ecstatic sea of divine unity.

You are what you are seeking!

CHAPTER 22
Crystalline Energies

Aros, today 50 years ago in your time language you crystallized your energies to become a human form, in what you call taking birth. This allows us the excellent opportunity to expand more on energy and its movement. We, the Comet so to speak, are celebrating you on this day together with the Whales and dolphins and many of your wonderful and various teachers from different dimensions. Of course, the one you so lovingly like to call Baba and his successor Gurumayi and the entire lineage of light masters are very much part of this. Always remember the gift of receiving the mantra Om Namah Shivaya has also prepared you to tune into us and many other subtle energies that are your real and lasting energy blueprint. The mantra is continuing to support you in many different ways, which is not always so obvious. What is not understood by many, is that within the inherent vibrations of certain syllables, when consciously empowered by a true light being and the lineage of self-realized masters, a field of energy is created and released that will not be grasped by the mind and its purpose is to allow the mind to remember its true nature as divine consciousness and give up the idea that it is anything but consciousness. This realization is a movement of grace. The allowance of grace releases the light pattern that will start to vibrate at a certain frequency, which your intuition will comprehend as something it knows without knowing. In other words, in linear language, this can not be fully explained, because it is generated from a very different plane of consciousness. Nevertheless, your destiny on this planet is about to be fulfilled. Even though we know you have heard this for a long time, it is true! Do not get caught up in the appearance of the present situation, that you lose sight of the larger picture. All pieces are part of the same puzzle.

Aros Crystos

The ocean has many drops. Yet without considering the Ocean herself, it would be very challenging to understand one single drop and its relation to the Ocean, the true source of its existence. Be at complete peace and know in your heart, that everything you have felt and dreamt about is to become your path and radiant guide.

CHAPTER 23
Greetings from Destination Unknown Reality

Do you like our play with words? What else is it? At this time we, the so-called Comet, would like to address what is now being expanded upon and the new and challenging discovery in your sphere of consciousness, that we are now the fragment of a distant planet that blew up millions of years ago. Well, it certainly leads to an interesting conversation piece and again will take you away from understanding and addressing what this is truly all about. We want to say this to all of you.

It is time for the whole planetary consciousness to learn to discriminate, about what you want to make the truth look like and how it truly appears when you let go of trying to understand it from your limited intellect. If all of you could start to embrace the divine aspect of this, you would in a flash let go of old worn-out ideas. No matter how many fancy terms you use and complicated explanations in the name of your importance, it still will not explain anything. It will, as most things you for so long have held to be your sacred solution, only take you around and around in circles. Where are you heading with that? Nowhere! And your solutions become your confused state of being. Anyone who does not address this from a spiritual point of view will only lead you away and astray from the energy of your heart. We also know by studying the relationship between yourselves to the universe, that if the explanation is too simple, you will not believe it.

So many great beings that have trodden the soil of your planet, have all said the same, for eons now: you are the divine being, your path is oneness, your life is light and all your solutions are contained within the vibrations of your heart. We know that some of these messages will be displayed on the communication satellite, that you call the internet. We are pleased that aros has agreed to let it be so. At the same time, it is only the preparation for true communication. That, people of the earth, is the inner net!

Frankly, we, like many other beings and many parts of the universal consciousness, even though we care and love you unconditionally are slowly getting tired of repeating the same truth over and over again. Is there nobody on your planet in some sort of a government position, who dares to finally set this record straight?

Wars and politics create separation! The brotherhood of man creates unity and global abundance and prosperity.

We can now all start to enjoy and rejoice in the planetary shift of consciousness and support each other no matter what we look like, or where we come from.

It is that simple! Live it! Be it!

CHAPTER 24

Holograms!

What are they and how do they appear and why? We addressed it a little about it earlier and now we will dive deeper into it. A hologram is cells of energy immersed in a certain frequency, which creates the image of pictures in the third-dimensional consciousness. When we are saying immersed, we are referring to this from a spiritual understanding. Also, it would be next to impossible to understand it any other way. It relates to the fact that spiritual energies will not be trapped in a certain frequency. This allows them to freely interact with vibratory cell images. That, in turn, will create a super reaction of fine-tuned cells that can rearrange themselves in such a way that they can alter the frequency and, by that, the mode of behavior. That in itself creates the opening for a shift in reality. For example, in one single code the wonderful understanding of the existing perception of the blueprint for thousands of codes is contained, to rearrange themselves in a way that other dimensions can be perceived in the patterns of your evolutionary process. This may be at the beginning of the code, as it is surrounded by a vibratory frequency, somewhat foreign to itself. Nevertheless, the amazing thing is that it still opens the channels for certain images that have already been programmed into the equation and which you refer to as a hologram.

The reason for the name is that it is referred to as hollow. Being that it is not a solid substance and that it is free-flowing energy, it can be manipulated in such a way that it allows for the appearance of a limited and fearful concept, such as one that the human consciousness has been experiencing for eons now. In the past, that has been your truth and these different holograms have led you astray and away from discovering who you truly are.

CHAPTER 25
More Hale Bopp Transmissions

Aros, it is very close! Speaking: allow and let it be!

How you understand the illusion that we are appearing and disappearing right in front of you, is very much in tune with what we are sending out into the frequency of space to be picked up by the ones ready to hear it. It is indeed a complex and necessary hologram, which allows us and other star beings to operate undisturbed. One thing that we are creating is a giant hole in the time sequence of events. This allows slowly for the old hologram to be broken up and show you your true nature and the wonderful cosmic stage you are soon to act out upon in this sacred and mysterious play of the divine being.

We will address this matter more in detail at a later date. Right now we would like to continue on our original wavelength, about energy and its movement. As we mentioned before, the human body is created by a process of crystallization of certain energies.

The woman's body is created and developed to be able to facilitate this process. In other words, when a being is magnetized into a certain time element by creating contact between a male and a female, in an event you call making love, she becomes pregnant. It is rather important to understand that the process you call pregnancy, is not so much the fact that certain cells and chromosomes from the male are affecting the female by coming in contact with her. Rather it is the magnetic field that sets this process in motion. Then this field of super sensitive magnetics draws to itself all the inherent parts of the blueprint that has in its coding the program to become a human body. We are mentioning this, to make it very clear about the fact that speed transcends physical reality. For example, in taking birth the magnetic fields in a very natural way are manipulated to slow down the different components, cells, atoms, and so on, to become the body. When that takes place, the illusion of the physical is appearing. To use a simple analogy; like ice and water. What appears to be solid is nothing but liquid immersed in magnetic resonance. Take away the magnetics and what's left is the liquid special again. Another way to understand this is through movement. When any energy is slowed down, depending on how strong the magnetics are, this will determine what quality of physical substance will appear. Remember is it an appearance because the true substance is and will always be flowing energy. Now, to this equation add your understanding that the magnetic field around the planet is dropping away. What will this do to the appearance of physical reality, based upon the understanding that everything in its natural state is flowing energy and that it has been the magnetics that kept the illusion in place?

Yes, it is an awesome realization and the possibilities are truly endless. You are more poetically once again becoming part of the divine breath. We would truly suggest that all of you contemplate this and allow this to become part of every cell of your being. To be alive on a physical planet in such a transformation is no less than a glorious moment in the time of galactic evolution.

CHAPTER 26
What is Energy?

It is moving particles programmed into an evolutionary pattern or grid, guided by a force field of magnetic resonance and substance. With all of this, we are attempting to explain something that can not be explained by your current understanding. It is rather an inner sensation, based upon that your consciousness has within itself the total equation of the totality of all that there is, at any given moment outside of time and space. We could complicate this by using a mathematical formula? We are here to take you out of the confusion and to avoid creating any more limiting concepts by the mind. At the same time, it is valuable to remember that some formulas are a true necessity to express and explain a certain sentiment about a state of being.

CHAPTER 27
Last Transmission & Acceptance

It is time to allow your life and the events, both spiritually and materially, to happen within the flow of acceptance. What does that mean? This means accepting that, whatever situation you seem to find yourself in, it is no more than that: a situation! It will allow you to be fully free to create whatever you want to accomplish. For whatever reason, that energy is not different from the place we are operating from.

As we are approaching your planet in a physical sense, we are at the same time allowing the energy of acceptance to be present within our consciousness, so that all of you will be able to tune into our wavelength. This creates the opening for the mass consciousness to be in the clear and wonderful realization. If you allow the energy of full acceptance to be present, this in itself allows for the magnificent opening of the truth of full understanding. We, the Comet, are fully aware of many different levels of your belief system and your subtle understanding of the universe and the acceptance of other life forms. That allows us to adapt to the situation at hand.

When you learn to understand and accept with no restriction, you allow for a transformation to take place. That is why we have waited with many other star beings to fully become present within your time and space. We have, in many different ways, been preparing you to accept us and our approach into your time continuum. So you, in turn, will allow yourself to understand us with love and honor our presence here in your plane of existence. We can tell you that this preparation has been in many ways a long road. Nevertheless, many of you are now aware of the fact that there are enough of you, who have raised your vibration level to be able to once again embrace other universes and beings from other planets and other realities, that the masses are not aware of yet. This activation is now creating the space for a full ignition of your inside being and all its treasures and gifts. The irony is, that what used to keep you from experiencing your multidimensional being is now becoming your solution and your path to freedom. In this hologram more and more humans will start to recognize us, as something different from a Comet, not knowing what they perceive us to be. Yet there is the real feeling that we are not what they have been led to believe. That opening creates the opportunity for us to communicate on wave frequencies that carry in themselves the vibration of communication, which allows us to be fully present to all of you, who we truly are, and our purpose to be visiting you at this delicate time in your evolution. This might be important when you witness us in your physical sky. Reflect on this simple yet profound truth and observation.

How is it possible for you to see us and at the same time believe that we are just a piece of rock, soaring through your physical space? Because remember, what you normally do not believe, you will not perceive.

It is only possible because we are allowing your perception to be altered. To recognize something that you do not quite understand. This is only possible because of what we referred to earlier; that there are enough humans who have owned up to the intriguing possibility that what used to be their belief system and survival is now falling apart.

Their truth is being challenged in every aspect of their life. The solution can only be found in a different understanding altogether. The amazing aspect of this is, that it only takes one sincere human, with absolute faith and the right understanding to allow his mind to accept us fully who we are and what we are. The result of this will allow us to beam crystallized electrons into your consciousness. It will allow the perception to be altered in such a fashion, that in a very natural way, the wave scanners of your brain will start to scan for an opening to empower, in this case, an electromagnetic thought to beam itself beyond your stagnant belief system. This is the work and preparation many of us have been doing to facilitate this process, not with only one single thought, but with the entire range of your belief system.

We are truly pleased to inform you that it is almost done. We will now activate this new understanding. Then we will be able to appear in your physical consciousness, with many other star-beings, that equally have been preparing and waiting for this time to arrive.

No more hide and seek, so to speak.

We will be appearing in our natural glory and now you will be able to shine with us.

Yes, we know, of course, what the next restriction from some of your learned ones would be. It is the light from the sun and self-generated gasses that makes us visible, right? wrong! How could the sun possibly be the agent that allows us to appear in your evening sky?

Aros detected us in full sunlight on Maui in a place above the clouds.

Reflect on this and keep in mind, if it was that simple, what about all the other objects that are constantly rushing through your physical space? Or do most of your educated minds believe that comets and asteroids only appear once in a while? That would be the same as saying that the wetness of the ocean is only there once in a while. The ocean is of course always wet, even if someone would come up with some new way of looking at it, the answer will still be the same. As a matter of fact in this case the ocean is not even aware of the turbulence its natural state is creating. In the same way, the universe no matter how you look at it or understand it, is always full of particles like the kind of asteroids and comets and other natural debris arriving and appearing, because of the evolution of the material universe. It is truly very natural and quite common.

Once again; the only reason you can see us is because we have altered our intens- frequency, in such a way that you will perceive us as bright shining light, nothing to do with the sun. Also remember, that we are arriving out of another time continuum altogether, because of this alteration of frequency. You can at least accept us as something bright in the sky. If we did not do this, you would not be able to perceive us at all. We would be like a cloaked spaceship, right there among you and yet not visible to you. Understand and remember that your so-called history has been altered and changed to manipulate and control and keep your consciousness in a vibration of lower understanding.

As long as your people, whoever they are, keep persisting on that track of limitations, they will never, so to say, catch the train. It will always delude them. Your future science will not be born out of the education of past control and manipulation. It will be brought into its true alignment by people who have no real education because the truth does not require books and schools to be understood.

What it does require is self-generating understanding, which comes when the heart is vibrating in tune with the rhythm of the divine soul. That is the real school of the future; to be able to be so in tune with the vibrations of the heart, that everything is there without looking for it.

That is the same as embracing the totality of the moment generated by the exquisite feelings of unity in all things and everything. Then our appearance and others like us, would not even be a consideration or a question. It would be natural and in complete acceptance of the wonderful enfolding of your universal frame of reference based upon the divine heart, simple and clear and only full of ecstasy in all its aspects

CHAPTER 28
Orchestra of the Universe

Listen, listen to the orchestra of the universe! Follow our dance and our sound of divine freedom. Allow yourself to merge into the infinite music of transformation emitting from the stars. The beginning and the end are merging into the eternal moment and the time of deep transmigration is here to be fully embraced. Behold the bell of joy and the infinite treasures that are sung by us, whales and dolphins, and serenaded in the eruption of nature's divine gifts.

Wisdom and love are there to be seen and understood in the light of clarity. There the dagger of duality is cut in two by the sword of discrimination. In that energy light upon light is being transmitted to the heart of humanity.

Listen! Learn! And trust! The elixir pouring out from the pitcher, held by the ecstatic lover, is filling all of your beings and allowing the path you tread to be light and oh, so sweet. As you taste its sacred ambrosia, all doubts vanish from your cells, and left is only the pulse of the everlasting smile of us, the dolphins, and our sacred rhythm of sound, serenading and celebrating the divine play of creation. Listen! Listen! Listen!

Dolphin Transmissions

You will have the opportunity to come and play with us. Then you will be healed. You are bold and courageous and we, as ancient beings, honor that very much, because that is what foundations are built upon. be aware of the people that are coming into your life from now on. Some of them will play a major role in your new life experience in the light.

We love you and send you vibrations that will heal and support you.

The sounds of the waves are calling you to us. Listen and respect your true values.

Indeed that was the beginning of my life with the dolphins and their energy, needless to say, it has been and is an amazing adventure that I embarked upon and the dolphins are playful teachers yet with an edge that has pushed me at times into a very different vibration and understanding.

Sacred Clown,

What is a sacred clown? An intricate way of releasing a light beam through the amusing awareness of a clown. In the Hopi traditions, the sacred clown is a shaman and a high priest who teaches by doing the opposite and they are considered to be holy men.

When the cells are infused by light, our awareness will shift on all levels, and we will once again see ourselves as loving light, as love and laughter.

When that takes place, the cells will start to vibrate at another frequency, and in that vibration old negative patterns are exposed and catapulted out of the system. It could be compared to the way a spacecraft moves into hydrospace by its creation of propulsion speed.

As dolphins and whales, and other advanced beings have become significant symbols in the way we are using our sonar and our pure intent when we want to penetrate the physical senses and matter and recreate it, once again, into flowing energy. The way we use our healing power is not different.

Truly light beings are only as bright as the image they have of themselves.

Ancient Formulas

This is the epoch for the truth to erupt and make itself quite clear in your life. Ancient times are coming to fruition. The symbol of the King and the Princess of Lemuria and Atlantis is emerging again and the ancient ways of wisdom and grandeur are there for humanity to behold in their relationship with themselves.

Let go! Let yourself drift into our cellular wavelengths and allow that feeling to become like a chariot that will take you very deep into your being.

These revelations are transmitted on a wavelength that will be your true channel for receiving the many messages that your mind and heart must transmit and translate into human understanding. In this frequency, many of us, like dolphins and whales are generating certain information through our interactions that is creating a holy grid, an accurate divine web of sacred interstellar information, that you will be prepared to transmute into precise holograms. These will create a pattern that will allow the individual consciousness to be linked into the holy matrix hidden within the constellations of the stars and their true origin. The mathematical formula that is described in all of the scriptures, is decoded in a circle of vibrations.

Always remember that the divine being would not allow for the creation of an entire scripture of information without hiding the real truth and at the same time its interpretation to be available to those who are ready to hear it. Another way of saying this, no matter how it has been manipulated, the revelations that need to be revealed have been manifesting in a complete and accurate order of understanding. It is the vibrational code of the words that allows you to find the divine key to the mystery.

Unified Field

Ultimately! Since there is only one truth, we are one unified field of energy, interacting with each other on many different levels of understanding. Thus we are creating a certain vibrating frequency, which in turn gives us our experience of life.

Therefore whatever you judge someone else, you ultimately do to yourself. To overcome this and change those patterns, your experience of existence must be aligned with the quantum possibilities of what light or consciousness is, not only seen from your limited concept or belief system. In short, as you change your field of perception of what the truth is all about and allow it to expand and become more flexible, your frame of reference will also change. This will allow for a deeper understanding of the experience you call life and all the players as part of the play. Then when you reach the point of clarity, that unity is always vibrating in your awareness. Have the faith and courage to act out of that space. Your experience of life will be one of complete harmony and unity. Then all the players will be seen and understood as your divine reflection.

When you participate in someone else's success with this frame of understanding, you draw this success into your own experience like a magnet. Then in your flow of life, you can recognize easily that in the polished mirror of understanding all injustice, fear, and anger will drop away like ripened fruit on a tree. The branches of that tree will grow out of perfect balance based on consciousness and its true source.

Before you might have used the word challenge to be able to activate this and now you will use the word solution. There the past and the future are mirrored in the giant kaleidoscope seen through the big now. When you allow this understanding to be present all the time, you will come to recognize that it is a question of substance and not about form and shape, also the subject and the object will vanish. It could create the clear, wonderful insight that when humanity at large embraces this with love and acceptance, out of that energy a whole new awareness will be born. This will align your life experience, merging out of the cocoon into remembering your true source and your universal heritage, that you are truly one divine being, sharing the same journey and adventure.

This could also easily be expanded upon with the analogy of how an ice cube might feel separated from its source, water! In the same way, all of you have felt separated from consciousness. Finally, the now has arrived, when you are shifting your perception from feeling like an ice cube to flowing water. The energy that is once again pouring out of your heart will melt your limited awareness and allow you to merge back into the eternal river of love and light.

Our imagined separation will be dissolved in the eternal moment in our evolution into the waters of bliss and ecstasy.

CHAPTER 29
Glide Gracefully into the 5th Dimension

We are preparing all of you to glide gracefully into the fifth dimension.

The new dawn and era that Mother Gaia is preparing for are approaching rapidly. Part of the truth is that all the events and the intricate formations and changes it carries with them have already taken place. At the same time, these events are allowing the breakup and disappearance of old worn-out patterns once and for all. In short, the entire atmosphere around the planet is being infused with a new and higher frequency that will heal and replenish the mass consciousness.

The sacred Hawaiian Islands! In their energy, they have the blueprint of being a gateway into the fifth dimension and the interstellar gateway to dimensions within dimensions.

In all of your journeys, always remember the sacred heart of the Hawaiian islands and allow yourself to tune into that energy and honor the islands in this way. In this wonderful shift, a new species is being born out of the divine memories in the human soul.

"The waters are sacred of its natural honesty. Its inhabitants will naturally inherit this quality.

As the sun slowly rises and embraces the ocean and as the dawn is taking the place of the echo of the night, in the same manner, will our hearts first embrace ourselves and then the entire universe, because an ocean of water starts with a single tiny drop. So does the merging into our truth start with a single breath? In that joyful moment, the leap of the dolphins is truly the magic rising of the divine energy, reaching up and beyond the created universe.

Hearts merge into hearts, hands holding hands creating a bond. Eyes meeting eyes beholding eternity. Wholeness is a single moment of peace. The dolphins!

The Galactic Command

Your music and voice will truly echo through the human consciousness, yes indeed you will be well known, and not only because of your voice, but it is also more than the divine frequencies coming through you will enable divine memories to emerge and be remembered by the ones listening

Crop Circles are dimensional gatherings once you perceive the earth again from a fifth-dimensional point of view, you will come to recognize that the entire planet is infused and made up out of sacred symbols. In essence, what is taking place with the crop circles and the white lights appearing before the formation of the symbols, if you like the white lights are like the guardians as well as the ones that manifest the circles. Commander as you are well aware something like this is not happening the way it looks as it does. This is an immediate interplay within the dimensions of physical reality and much more subtle planes of existence. Beloved Aros, perceive it with this understanding that it is all flowing energy and that all the sacred signs appearing are also overlapping each other within this flow and are constantly moving like rings and ripples on the water. The white lights know how to pull and draw certain messages taking the forms of crop circles out from their fourth and fifth-dimensional existence and then pulling them into your third-dimensional physical awareness.

It is also wise to remember that all dimensions are entwined with each other, like threads in a garment, and everything and anything ever been created is ultimately always flowing energy and because of that what is perceived as a crop- circles is a direct link to the evolution of human consciousness. In short, as the earth is changing its frequencies and people are awakening the magnetic resonance within the consciousness is drawing to itself these images, all this will lead to a recall of the divine origin within the human consciousness in the divine evolution. The human body is made up of the same material substances as the earth, so the earth in many ways is always mirroring inside the human body her expansion and of different frequencies. That is why at times people see and recognize these various symbols because they are awakening from within and are seeing the mirror. From our vantage point, it is truly interesting to observe that among all your wars and tumult, fears, and manipulation that so many are distancing themselves from a described reality and are finding a new way to perceive and understand themselves and the world they live in, and also Aros you and many others how your merging is quite similar to the construction of light encodings in their merging to become the Mothership with many of her star beings of service to the adventure and the light it carries. Commander the impatience and at times the turbulent energy you are feeling and the new direction you are being asked to be part of are the energies that are holding the reins to the chariot, and this is all part of the warrior energy being released so you can fulfill your life and projects in the focus of a laser beam and with the strength and flexibility of the wind. Remember this! It's the same wind that touches you wherever you are on the planet, in the same way, your life is a dance of divine madness, the same energy that moves through the elements. Any kind of success will be looked upon in the same way as the elements are always interacting and sharing themselves.

This formula is magic and not yet opened or understood by humanity, it is a very honorable and special gift. It is a divine mirror that all things are possible in the erupting energies that are creating the adventure of searching for the answers on the stage of making belief. Such a true delight to be in the clarity that the one creating and searching and the one finding are the same. Of course, commander, this play will always and continuously be part of the adventures in consciousness and in a way will never see completion. New beginnings? absolutely and within the spectrum of knowing, that the truth is always ready to bear witness to itself, with joy and laughter and supreme humor in its divine theatre of make belief.

Back into the Stars again!

The false understanding about Christ and his mission and crucifixion will be laid to rest and free the human consciousness to remember and by that understand who Christ is and was and his purpose on this planet. Your body is like a building, before it was separated into different doors and windows and entrances. Now the building will be a perfect mirror of your soul and all parts of your inside and outside will shine in the brilliant light. The separation of the body, mind, and soul will unite as one truth and one path. This will lead as well to telepathic communication and you stand in your truth as a bright shiny light and a witness to the saying, that God dwells within the human heart. Diving into the abyss will now become a wondrous adventure and you will join whales and dolphin energies as well as ascended masters connected to the multi-faceted diamond of ancient temples of real resurrection. Your life will be like sensual lovemaking in the ether and eternal nights of remembering the sun shining in every cell and atom of your being. Your experience is nearing its completion and your time of putting on the crown is at hand not to be denied. The king on the inside will merge with the one on the outside and you will bear witness to how your light is manifesting here on this planet and you will carry the torch of divine transformation across the world. You will be seen and revered as a great master and your name Aros Crystos will be spoken on many lips We are now sharing this with you as you are now ready to establish your kingdom in this world again, because your energies are now matching your divine purpose as you are not controlled anymore by human emotions and the pair of the opposite.

CHAPTER 30
The Elementals

Jubilations, truly the different strands of energies, are unfolding themselves to create a wide web of intergalactic formations in the ever-expanding circus of divine theater and the ever-alive multidimensional patterns you are following. It is a divine adventure supported by being in clarity how vital it is to be bold, kind, and gentle and at the same time disciplined enough to show strength being forceful when it calls for that energy and to remember within the knowing, it is all part of perfect love and it's the truth of expressing itself. This is the crowning of many crystal light stars of dimensional encodings that originated from the light of holographic universes contained within all dense matter and divine substance. We are the elementals, and it seems that our dwellings are within all rocks and stone formations, yet that would be like saying the sun's rays are stuck in a pool of water and that the sun lives in the reflection she is dancing upon. Our purpose is to bring about the reawakening of the magical nature of a universe forlorn and forgotten in the web of fear and separation in the human mind and its dormant awareness of what is divine consciousness. We are the cross-bearer of pure wisdom of old lands and kingdoms and only partly remembered in some of your folktales and fairy tales of old. Where do we exist? We could be seen as the mirror of what is, and what will be again. We are also the healing power and remedy of a long-forgotten art.

Commander, you are now accessing something we call the vacuum between different states of consciousness. We are in deep gratitude to you for accepting this mission as it will change many things all around you, maybe more quality is the beautiful fact that it will allow you to tap into and draw from the radiant flowing inspiration of abundance.

You use the electromagnetic energies behind any thought, negative or positive with no attachments that will in turn open up a tunnel for the consciousness to travel through, similar to a black hole in the universe. The vacuum generates the speed for this to take place. The outcome is that you can use energy in a very powerful and creative way. Before it might have been that certain energies were using you, but not now, you will be if you like the conductor of the music. This is vital as it creates a space for you to travel in and out of various realities, similar to how the dolphins travel through portals in the ocean. This is the launching pad and the galactic code of inherited master builders of super sensitive electrons in the blueprint of the galactic master and his command in the evolution of transforming the human consciousness back into infinite openings and possibilities. This will lead you to see and understand a dramatic shift in the blueprint, originating from the cosmic unfoldment in galactic evolution.

The Galactic Federation

Awakening from the deep slumber in the cocoon of forgetfulness and breaking into the crisp new dawn takes courage, right faith, clear thinking and trust in a very different world from the one promoted to keep you in forgetfulness of your true nature. We are mentioning this because this plays a vital part in the awakening of the human consciousness and what they are being guided to follow and accept unconditionally, as this new world will be the one that will provide clues and guidance and deeper understanding to follow. The old ways are truly like a dying dinosaur and any history that is based upon that linear timeline is disappearing in that bright new awareness. The ones that are still choosing to hold on to the old ways, such foolishness, we will certainly not waste time on that. Life is always experienced through different openings in the energy spectrum 'of make belief' in the dream of illusion and separation. When you let go, it can feel like the earth underneath your feet is vanishing and you are suspended in mid-air. That allows the consciousness like a king awakening from a dream to question what is real and what is a dream. In the dream, he was a beggar, and now awake he is laying in his royal bed with his servants fanning his heated body and his ministers ready to answer every question. He realizes that neither his dream nor this awakening state is different, they are both real and unreal, and with newfound clarity, he can recognize that all this, is his divine intelligence playing with itself as the world and the universe and in truth his entire kingdom with all its people and servants like a painted picture. Nice to behold and not real and there is no one else except this divine self, playing hide and seek with itself as the universe. Aros like the King you are embracing yourself as a true emperor of your divine creation all the different incarnations in multifold universes, and epochs will lose their grip on you and return to their natural state of flowing energy. You may be visible to the people on earth, and yet far beyond comprehension.

A Spectrum of Possibilities

Within the spectrum of possibilities is a built-in understanding and an opening for instant change and alteration of any situation. The overtone of the adventure will remain in harmony with the delicate outcome already described in countless volumes through epochs in the human saga and its expansion into divine unconditional love and light of the true destiny of planet Earth as she soars into the new galactic frequency in the abundant discipline of knowing the divine outcome before it was even written as a possibility in the consciousness of mankind. Your adventure commander here on this planet will certainly be engraved into the matrix in the new human imprint and will be remembered and have a lasting impact on the evolution of the human consciousness for a long time to come.

Beloved one, light beams of radiation of the purest energy of transformation within the clear substance of illusion in the highest order of supreme advancement of the nectar of spiral crystals on the ladder of the organization of the pattern within the delicate codes, that are creating the new fine-tuned balanced hologram. In the human saga, a new understanding is being birthed from the foundation of pure and exuberant love in the emergence of the radiant truth of all dimensions and levels, radiating from the deep seeded divine original transformation from the source of all creations. Beloved Aros, as you can see and experience, the way we are now communicating with you and the language will resonate from an activation point from the purest radiation beams as you have now emerged to embrace your divine adventure in somewhat of a different understanding, and by activating these ancient resonances of supreme knowing are now being transmitted from the Mothership into you. The feeling of being left here and being alone in this very confusing reality will be no more as it is not part of your reality, your life can only now be experienced as truly divine, whatever it might be and was earlier felt like trivial and mundane is now being expressed from the new infusion of crystal clear understanding. Only beings that are resonating within this frequency can be part of your life and your communication spectrum. Another way of explaining this divine commander, many parts of your own divine self from various epochs and adventures in time, are now returning in a tangible way to assist you.

CHAPTER 31
Sonic Codes

What is happening to my voice? The dolphins, dear one, we had to shut you down for a while to be able to do an energetic surgery on your vocal cords, so they can vibrate at a much higher frequency and also create an opening for various beings to express themselves through you. The work and fulfillment of your vibrant destiny are partly contained within your vocal cords. As you perform the Sonic Codes and share the tones and the vibration emitting from you, it will align people's physical and emotional bodies in perfect harmony. Imagine as you become more aware of your strengths and how to use your power with divine purpose and frequency. As you delegate command the tone of your voice will create clarity and acceptance. Instead of hearing only the words and their drama, they will be able to feel and experience the purpose of their divine unfoldment. No more personal investment! The crystalline energies of the liquid pyramid that we are installing in your voice will be powerful indeed. Your voice will become a divine tool and instrument. For this to take place you had to come to a certain understanding within yourself. The sound and tones you sometimes hear in your ears and feeling blocked is part of the adjustment to be able to hear and adjust to higher frequencies. The pituitary and pineal glands are as well being activated. The feeling that started over 20 years ago about the experience that your entire being was being dismantled and put back together again, this as well as part of the divine completion. You will be able to listen and communicate with all of nature and the elements, this will be as natural as the divine breath. In the inhalation breathe in the life force and in the exhalation let the life force be expanded until your mind becomes still. In the out-breath, you are truly touching home. This conscious breathing practice will align the body as divine alchemy is happening inside. The crystals energy of coded electrons that are vibrating within the flood of your blood and on a cellular level changing the crystal coded to respond to a different set of references, every cell, and every organ will vibrate to the tune of your voice. You will be able through your voice, sweet Aros command any part of your body. What we are conveying here is the human voice, when understood, can affect and create openings for healing, and stilling the mind and have a positive effect on your whole life. Similar to the dolphins, how they use their pure intent and sonar to create healing energies and transformations in people's lives. They operate from the premise that every organ is like a musical instrument and for everything to be aligned with the music, every instrument has to be in tune with each other and if one piece is out of tune it affects the entire composition and so as well in your body. Quite astonishing, yes we would say so, this is the natural state of affairs of the royal imprint in the galactic unfoldment inscribed within each human being's destiny on this planet and beyond. The adventure of the self and its self-discovery to remember never ends and every new revelation and insight is a stepping stone and activation point to another interstellar portal. The awakening from deep slumber must be achieved with royal steps, meaning the quality of nobility, truth, and respect for one's self is a must otherwise the opposite could be activated and come into play and by that a platform for the ego to use this information to launch you into a very different set of circumstances, that will take you further away from the truth and the ability to recognize what is true and what is not. The voice will return in a couple of days and the pressure in the ears will as well be gone. Here I like to point out that after this incident, my voice came back with another frequency and power and it showed up very soon when I went back to my healing sessions. One woman in Columbus shared with me that as I was working on her she opened her eyes and I had shape-shifted into a dolphin.

The Power of Vulnerability

Dear Aros, you can understand the winds of change are upon the land and, they will carry in their embrace powerful transformative eruptions within the human psyche. We are listening to your heart, dear friend and as the energy of the dolphins, we are always eager to share with you the sensation of the merging truth in all its shapes and forms. Truly being vulnerable is such a rare gift and almost forgotten within the human equation, it can be a sacred pillar to build upon because no one can truly strive to become all there is without letting go of the imaginary armor that has been like a heavy door shut to your heart. Vulnerability is a fresh aroma carried by gentle winds across the land of intimacy and vulnerability. It is a gift indeed. As you inhale this nectar you will experience true intimacy cherished by the gods of change. Your heart is the true alchemy of intimacy and in that space of vulnerability, all illusions drop away. These feelings of not being enough or feeling unworthy and the sensation that you have to become something will melt away with the sweet and enduring kiss of intimacy. True intimacy is to be free of all shame and guilt and when that happens you can truly live, love, and experience every moment as sacred worship of the divine and recognize and embrace that every form and shape is the perfect manifestation of the formless presence within your being. This as well empowers you to listen beyond the sound of your voice, it will empower you to hear beyond the hearing and will remind you that true listening is the vibrant formation of generous playful clouds, playing in the breath of the absolute and the dynamic embrace of cosmic energy and inhaled by the divine goddess in her search of her divine lover Listening, intimacy, and vulnerability, are infinitely entwined like the wind and its movements, like perfume and its aroma, like fire and heat and like a reflection in the mirror. Because of that as you completely embrace and allow yourself to be dressed in one of these treasures the others will follow as night follows day and as a storm cleans the air and as the sun teaches you to appreciate both sun and shadow. Beloved it's a miracle, behold it and let gratitude guide you in gratitude for all the precious gifts you are receiving.

The cross will come down and the crucifixion will be a legend not remembered. The inhalation of pure consciousness with every breath will become the next symbol of freedom. You have come from a world far beyond this one. You have come to establish the rich and abundant kingdom of the emperor of all kingdoms. Your journeys and adventures have been long and challenging, your energies will be forever engraved in the human consciousness. Trust in the rhythm of your heart and allow this dance to take your final steps toward liberation and as you do the portal for liberation for the human consciousness will be flung wide open.

Wisdom is the absence of knowledge!

CHAPTER 32
Nothing is as it seems

Ambassador, in the reality of light-filled universes unfolding within a tiny blue star of supreme consciousness. What seems to be not real at times, remember is still part of a larger truth within the light-filled matrix of pure consciousness that can reveal itself in an instant and alter anything in the physical universe. Commander, we are always protecting and honoring your sacred duty and commitment to at times seemingly impossible adventures on this planet. All we ask of you is to keep your trust in what you know to be so and the result of this mission, truly the next part of your mission has already been written and in many ways manifested already and the triumph will finally be yours to behold and also the crowning moment of countless missions here and may other realities and star systems.

Activation Portal Through Syllables

Activation portals through syllables. Yes, absolutely commander, from Eros to Aros and from Christos to Crystos. It is truly like walking through a dimensional portal, this example is very real because there is always a magnetic activation point upon which the setup for a special activation will be focused. In this part of the adventure Aros, it has been wonderful to observe as the energies of Aros started to create a matrix while you were still hanging on to the energy of Eros. The energy of Eros in this case represented the third dimension and Aros the fifth dimension. Certainly! The geometric formation has been a guiding sign on your path to remember. There is now an opening that can allow for the realization that the human consciousness can be part of your various projects. Sometimes we refer to you as a child. It is a symbol of the radiance of a galactic ray that carries in its energy truth and splendor born from innocence. Innocence is the real understanding of how to perceive the seed of creation and creation itself. In innocence, there is tremendous potential for divine portals to be activated.

Mystical Doorways!

Amazingly, I asked the love birds for a message, vulnerability, intimacy, and listening. The next moment, Professor Robert is laying on the floor and gestures for myself and Moon to do the same. Robert has taken over the situation and is guiding us both in our interaction with each other and she was sharing that she felt uncomfortable and insecure when she was around me. I at that moment choose to surrender to my vulnerability and she continued that a few days ago when I had channeled at the Dolphin House she could not sit still and was judging and at the same time had the longing that she could be as vulnerable as Juliana and Mary-Joe and be in that peaceful state and she felt that they experienced great joy. She did admit that most of the time though, she had been out and could not remember what took place. Moon I asked, somewhat confused, if this is how you are feeling why did you agree and be open to promoting my work here in your place Mystical Doorways, and also otherwise? She answered that my experience with you is that at times you are not in touch with your heart and because of that you keep people at a distance that truly wanted to share with you from a deeper place, and at the same time I recognize something in you that is so much greater. When we went to the Indian powwow I felt how you opened up and allowed your vulnerability to come out. Your heart was open and it was a delight to spend time with you. The three of us are still on the floor and Robert asks me, how many women I kept at a distance. A few I answered. at that moment I had the courage to be completely vulnerable because of the guidance from Robert, I could recognize through the veil of denying that as a part of Christ, I had closed my heart to the energy of Mary Magdalene and the roles we had chosen to play in this galactic event in history and at times this was more painful than the entire episode so long ago. When I had gone to the jungle to cry out and release this unbearable intense energy and to find clarity about the relationship. Most of this part has never been understood because of its simplicity, something humanity could not accept. Here I need to intervene, that when I am talking about Christ I am talking about the consciousness that many of us experienced in those days and also the cosmic Christ, Sunanda who is truly a Starbeing and not the Carpenter. Apparently, two beings were playing this role. So historians did what has been done so many times throughout history, making it much more complex and confusing. A king would never be caught barefoot, always in royal attire. Because of this most of the real meaning and simplicity was lost. I had at some point chosen to close my heart to love and intimacy on the physical plane. This matrix has been with me for a very long time and no wonder I was so intent to bring down all physical crosses and so the real message of unity within the male and female got lost and never quite understood instead more separation was created and through the centuries, the playfulness of relationships was lost and replaced with the battle of the sexes. laying there on the floor with moon and Robert I felt like I had been crucified over and over again, I started to cry gently. I understood my destiny and that all the players were being gathered together again to celebrate and create the deliverance from all this false and separate understanding. Now! It was about the healing of human consciousness by merging the male with the female from within. The resurrection of true understanding. It was an awkward moment for sure to become aware of this in that environment, the puzzle pieces of this giant puzzle called life had been scattered everywhere and now they started to fit together. Empowered by Robert I sat up and held Moon in my arms as my divine sister representing the Mother Mary energy. I have missed and longed for my brother for such a long time, we were both ready to heal these wounds carried through many incarnations. She looked into my eyes and expressed what she saw. The truth! Like myself, she was letting all the tension go and she as well looked more approachable. We had both heard the message from the love birds, they had been silent when these revelations took place and as if they were listening to every word, then suddenly they started to sing again as a confirmation of what had taken place. Robert and I were holding Moon's hands and I felt real and very vulnerable and intimate and was listening to my heart. I felt that I was being released to be able to continue and do my work here on this planet. I had gained peace and truth and was ready to be and express who I truly am. A few moments later I was sharing how I got the name, Christos, and the light went out and came back on another sign. Something dropped from my arms and fell on the floor. Robert commented, let it all go, all the garbage you have been carrying around with you. Baba Muktananda used to say I am a garbage collector, give it all to me.

I felt at that moment clear about many of my relationships, and various women had played their part in bringing about these revelations and finally set people free from still hanging on the cross and instead focus on the merging of the male and female within themselves. Christ would merge with his beloved and a new era of the Goddess era had begun. I shared that Lynn the woman I had met In Mount Shasta when listening to a talk from Sunanda by a woman who channeled that energy. I had driven up to Mount Shasta with 3 other women, one of them was from the Pleiades, and when she had met me sometime earlier, she started to cry and took me to Kinko's to copy something and when she shared with me the photo and I compared it to one I had of myself, we looked like brothers and she told me this is Ashtar my father and I was her brother and I did not remember much of this and at times she got very agitated that I could not recall my other lives, that she seemed to remember so well. I used to Channel the Ashtar Command and then later changed it to my galactic Family, the name was misused by another group. We arrived in MS from San Francisco at six in the evening and we were all sharing one room they wanted to go and find a shaman they knew about, I was laying on the bed fully dressed, and then around midnight I hear them coming back and I still fully dressed, very unusual that I was still on the bed as I do not sleep many hours. In the morning we compared notes. They told me that they did not find the Shaman and then several hours passed and they had no idea what happened. I said, well I was going to get up when you left and the next thing I know I am still on the bed six hours later. One of them said I remember now I was dreaming and Aros you were on the Mothership explaining the science of the ship and you spoke in a foreign language and then I woke up and you were still sleeping and kept talking in this language. We left Mount Shasta early about 2 am the following day and I was driving except for a glorious display of the night with thousands of stars it was dark and suddenly this golden light flashed over the car and I saluted and knew my family had visited us and taken us to the mothership and now they left.

A month later I was rather bored in Novato California and called Lynn and asked what are you up to. Nothing really, so we decided I would come for a short visit. She lived out in nowhere man's land, and the first thing I said to her. was" why Are you hiding"? A few weeks later the roof collapsed and she had to move and then the next thing I said, you are Mary Magdalene. It's worth mentioning here that I was not a follower of Mary Magdalene and I always saw her as a great saint and completely misunderstood in history. I admired her and her courage. At that instant, though, it was crystal clear that her energy was facilitated by Lynn. She anointed my feet and did another sacred ceremony not to be shared here. Sometime later she called me and said, I was in the shower and received the message to tell you to use Christos after Eros. She had appeared for a short time to bring these messages to me and then she vanished from my life.

Dear reader, remember we are still on the floor in Open Doorways. Robert said, now anoint the moon's feet and I kneeled and kissed her feet. She then revealed something rather sacred ."A friend of mine had met this man at Gentle Winds, that is where I was doing my healing work through Sonic Codes, she continued sharing, he was the first person in this lifetime she would bow down to. He is a great master. Moon then folded her hand together and said, you are that man, then she added maybe you have heard something like this before and yet this time now, it is very different. I answered that is why it was easy for me to bow down to you, Robert in his wise guidance added, you have now done that! Now recognize yourself as the master that you are. Moon the added you have been a king in many lifetimes, including in Atlantis. Writing these things down in Columbus and then later in Honolulu I had also digested all these experiences and knew in my heart and soul it was all true. "Baba said, only he who can obey can command and I think through the years of trials and tribulations I have finally learned this lesson and understand my destiny through this and other lifetimes and be at peace with it in the knowing that it is neither great nor not. It simply is, that awareness is very much portrayed by the dolphins in their behavior and how they interact. The early Essenes saw Christ as a Dolphin. Mother Mary means, born out of the sea.

CHAPTER 33
Multidimensional Soul

At some point, John Lennon became part of my life and when he was killed I was in Los Angeles, people came up to me, you are the living spirit walking around and at times it became too much for me as perfect strangers would approach me and tell me they are feeling his energy around me. I have never really understood the connection and did not allow myself to make anything out of it. I do think to some extent he and Yoko One did represent the merging of the Male and The Female on the physical plane.

I am now ready to command my fleet of starships again and as well be the captain of my soul. That is what God shared with me through this amazing man in Marbella in my Clothing Boutique, even though he could not hear or speak, through his drawing he spoke louder than any words and the two he did for me myself as Christ carrying the cross surrounded by women, he explained that I was carrying the world upon my shoulders and then like the Titanic standing in front of a large ship crossing the Atlantic with my arms stretched out. Returning captain of my own soul. He as well turned up out of nowhere to deliver this message and because of that I can now accept in myself what he saw in me already and with the grace of Baba and God, I was guided and looked after in sometimes not-so-obvious ways. The purpose will now be aligned with the divine matrix that I have carried in my being and I am now willing to let it replace itself as the new paradigm my soul has been waiting for. I am sharing this poem because as any one of us is awakening to the exquisite love inside of us, many new gifts will surface and life will take on a very different expression.

Aros Crystos

Victory to the Abundance of the Sacred Heart!

You have touched my heart with the sweetness of your being. The longing for you has been intense. Like a river flowing toward the ocean, so is my soul and entire being a flame of ecstatic love that wants to consume itself in your exquisite being. The stars and all the heavenly bodies rejoice in our merging hearts. Our bodies will be the sweet and tender reminder about the unfolding of our destinies as delightful filled pure radiant beings of light. As my mind and senses touch your beauty, it is filled with the reminder confirmation of a wonderful saga that had a bright shiny star as it's a poem. As we allow ourselves to merge into that promise of ecstatic surrender that was promised in another time and space. There the light of our oneness always filled the entire universe and where our shapes and forms was a lovely union of the beloved born by the rapture and tears of her divine lover. Truly sweet one, where is the difference between one single drop of the ocean and the ocean itself? Could or would the sun bear witness to its glory? The trees truly never eat their fruit. In the same way, you and I are the eruption of ecstatic divine love playing with itself to see itself. You are me and I am you. We are the promise of the union of all unions. We are the smoldering ember of all the fires that created this world. True words, true beauty, and true lives are filled with the adventure of being and not being. Listen! To these words of fulfilled ecstasy and know, as certain as the sun shines as its divine light, so are our hearts and the radiance from our souls its exuberant manifestation of divine light. The rapture and the ecstasy of the Goddess and her divine lover playing hide and seek for their divine pleasure in finding each other again and again and merging over and over again. The becoming is the orgasmic rapture of infinite love always taking complete delight in itself. These words are the mirror on a blank page, truly as the page wants to feel and experience itself the words become manifested and so is our truth and longing the dancing sensation of fully experiencing what we already are.

The truth manifests in divine ecstasy in infinite wisdom.

Love merges into Love.

My dear reader, I will continue with another poem that came through me when my heart and soul were freed from the layers of fear and separation. I am sharing this because you and I are not different, so in many ways what I am sharing with you is your adventure as well.

The Longing

I was longing for you, and suddenly in the world of confusion, you found me. Then there was laughter in my heart and a sweet mystery in my eyes. The longing and merging are flowing in harmony on the waves of pure ecstasy. The truth of being and becoming is melting into nothingness. I hear your voice from deep within my galactic soul, I have always been with you, and yet when I saw and touched you the first time I was filled and carried by the waves of deep gratitude. To hold you and kiss your soft waiting lips and feel your trembling body as it touches mine, is the legend of sweet miracles in the never-ending love of divine effulgence in the ecstatic ocean of bliss. My life has been a blur of distant secrets whispering and calling out to me from within the chambers of fear and separation. I knew that I knew, yet I was a prisoner of my self-created understanding to look for myself where I could not be found and then I saw the light in your eyes and all the false structures came tumbling down, and the orgasmic waters of pure radiant bliss was drowning me in sweet delight. I called out your name and through the distant epochs of my mind and traveling millions of light years, your voice was like ringing bells and tender laughter and I was free to love and behold my essence in your being, like a mirror looking at itself. I was open to seeing your infinite being and your beauty within myself and that you have been waiting patiently through countless creations to finally hear my voice calling out. waiting like a dry desert waiting to be graced by rain. Now when I look around, I see my divinity all around mirrored by your grace. Patience has its reward. I love you as my divine self and as my heart adores its rhythm. I love you as a tender memory of an infant remembering its divine father. I love you as only a being can that has been humbled by the search for the blossom of a flower of infinite nectar and joy in the garden of finite treasures.

Father Kuthumi!

Father Kuthumi speaking: You have come a long way and everything is happening in the way it was ordained. In a real sense what is happening has already happened. Aros, you are playing an important part in the evolving saga of reactivating the super-dynamic codes in the birthing of a new being. Be at peace as you will at times feel and experience the breaking up of the old paradigm and at the same time the sensation of merging is as well part of the new web being spun. Yes dear one, as you know Aros part of your job is to heal the fragmented parts of the Universe. This new web is very bountiful and beautiful spun by golden injections from a real and lasting understanding of who am I and what I am! Your life will be lived from the thread of divine light that will mend and heal the rip and tears in the web of possibilities for human evolution in divine consciousness.

Poems are not plagued by Time and Space

Years fade away in the bright shine of knowing. Knowing I am the eternal wisdom, I am the inspiration of dreams yet to come and be shared as the love of nature always gives away its delicious fruits and nectar. I am the bright new dawn of humble understanding born of the inferno of ecstasy in the lovemaking of time and space in the eternal wonder of make belief. Since I know this very instant, I am only playing a game with myself. I enjoy the wisdom and the beauty of my grace-filled years and I take delight in the joyous splendor that I was never born. I am and will always be the infinite exuberant and amazing play of light and dark in the forever brilliant womb of endless ecstatic possibilities nourished by millions of suns shining as infinite crystals in the divine heart of my divine self. I dance and celebrate my time on this earth and thank the energy of gratitude. I experience my life as a song and dance of the wondrous play of sweet duality in the merging waves in the ocean of eternity.

The Finale

The Sharing in this Book has only one purpose, it is to empower and encourage people to have the right understanding and see themselves as divine beings and pure consciousness. Never look upon yourself as small and insignificant and even in your ordinary life, make an effort to understand your life is a gift to remember and to be an expression of anything is possible when you live from your heart and trust in that vibration. You are certainly not here to only fulfill the longing of your senses and then die, no, you are here to paint your life as the most colorful and exciting piece of art and that living out of fear and separation takes you nowhere and instead replaces that feeling with I am perfect and whole this very moment and no one is more or less than anyone else and truthfully we are all masters playing with ourselves that we are here to remember that your lives are an expression from duality to unity and that everything we see and experience is through a giant mirror reflecting back at us, ourselves. You and I are divine consciousness now and forever more.

ABOUT THE AUTHOR

About Aros: From the depths of a small town in Helsingborg, Southern Sweden, emerged a profound question that would shape the very fabric of my existence. "Who am I?" These three words became the compass guiding my lifelong journey in pursuit of true understanding and wisdom. Without questioning, life lacks direction, and we risk becoming mere captives of other's ideas and perceptions.

At the tender age of sixteen, I embarked on my quest, resolute and unyielding, refusing to be defeated by anyone or anything until I had grasped the answer through personal experience. It is important to remember that when we dare to ask the right questions, we must also possess the unwavering faith to trust in the answers that unfold. Nearly six decades later, if I were to distill it all into one essence, I would declare that I walked a path only to realize there was never a path at all. For who I am now and forevermore is a radiant embodiment of divine consciousness.

Throughout the tapestry of my life, spirituality has been the guiding force, and my purpose has crystallized into awakening humanity to the profound truth that we are all interconnected as one divine consciousness. I am driven to assist individuals in rediscovering their true nature as divine, multi-dimensional beings. Through the gifts bestowed upon me, I express my creativity as a prolific writer, an artist of profound beauty, and a channel of healing sounds that ignite transformative experiences and elevate consciousness to higher realms.

As an intuitive coach and spiritual mentor, many seekers have sought out and benefited from the unique and potent gifts I offer. However, it is as an ambassador from the realm of dolphins that I find a special calling. Immersed in the vastness of the open ocean in Hawaii, I have spent years cultivating deep connections with dolphins and whales. In these sacred interactions, my multi-dimensional soul began to converse with me, delivering messages of profound beauty and wisdom that transcend the boundaries of ordinary existence.

With unwavering commitment, I now share my galactic heritage, illuminating the path for others to achieve a correct understanding of their true essence and untapped potential. Together, let us embrace the magnificent tapestry of our existence, for we are boundless beings, intimately connected to the infinite wonders of the cosmos.

About Radhaa Publishing House

Radhaa Publishing House is a rising star in the literary world, igniting the passions of authors and readers alike. With our commitment to excellence and dedication to storytelling, we have achieved numerous accomplishments that we proudly share.

We provide a platform for both established and emerging authors to share their voices and stories with the world. Our curated collection of diverse books, spanning various genres, has touched the hearts and minds of readers globally, inspiring profound transformations and sparking cross-border conversations.

At Radhaa Publishing House, we take pride in our meticulous editing, design, and production process, ensuring each publication meets a high standard of quality that resonates with readers and captures the essence of the author's vision.

Through our Author Incubators, Collaborative Books, and Sovereign Author Program, we nurture and support countless authors on their journey. Many of our authors have achieved international recognition, solidifying their place in the literary landscape and leaving a lasting impact on readers worldwide.

In addition to our publishing services, we offer comprehensive PR support to our esteemed authors. Crafting compelling press releases and facilitating media engagements, interviews, and collaborations, we amplify the reach of their literary works and help them connect with a wider audience.

By harnessing the power of strategic PR and media exposure, Radhaa Publishing House empowers authors to expand their reach, build their personal brand, and make a lasting impact. We believe that every author's voice deserves to be heard, and our PR services play a vital role in achieving that goal.

Aros Crystos

Our accomplishments in publishing and PR serve as a testament to our unwavering commitment to excellence and our belief in the transformative power of storytelling. Join us at Radhaa Publishing House and let your voice be heard as we continue to empower authors and inspire readers around the globe.

ABOUT RADHAA PUBLISHING HOUSE

BECOME AN AUTHOR
BECOME A CONTRIBUTING WRITER

Radhaa Publishing House is a holistic publishing company that focuses on helping heart-centered, mind-expanding, truth-telling authors get their work out into the world. Our focus is on collaborative book series and memoirs. We thrive on supporting our authors and contributing writers throughout this journey, empowering them to step into their divine and authentic voice while sharing their truth with the world. We especially celebrate cultural diversity worldwide, and we believe in weaving international voices to come together.

HOW ARE WE DIFFERENT?

Many collaborative publishing companies bundle the authors together so that they don't receive individual credit and acknowledgment. We make sure each Author is seen and heard and can be found easily. This has led to authors telling us that they have received more traffic and business and clients on their websites. In a sense, each of the Books we create is also like a Directory highlighting contributing writers' unique offerings. This has been a win-win for the contributing writers and authors.

Here is what our authors have said about working with us:

"I felt totally supported. The best bit was feeling like being part of a loving family who wants you to be your best, do your best, and is there for you every step of the way. It also boosted my confidence as a writer. The collaborative nature of the project also made it way more fun than doing things alone".

- Arrameia, Prague

"Visibility was a big piece of me coming out of the spiritual closet, and I felt that Radhaa Publishing House has a high energy and integrity level. Both of which are important for lightworkers and Starseeds. The curators and authors are light workers. Radhaa Publishing House created this wonderful opportunity for many others to be a part of. I felt that they put their whole heart into making this happen even before, during, and after the book is published. It was a project that was totally supportive that made me feel safe to share myself and my story." - **Lalitah, Turkey**

"It was wonderful to work with Radhaa Publishing House. I saw the effort and perseverance the whole team has and the support system they have for all the authors. I have matured as an author from this experience. I was so inspired after writing my chapter in this book, Awakening Starseeds, that I wrote an entire book called The Great Awakening because I was deeply moved by the writing."

- **Leshara, Philippines**

"My story was edited by Radhaa Publishing House, and let me tell you, it put me in tears! They made it better than the way I originally wrote and submitted it while keeping my story and voice true to its events. I read it, and tears just flowed because it was so good!"- **Cristal, Florida**

"I have published many books on Consciousness, empowerment subjects, and relationships, but I had never revealed raw, real stories of my life as with Awakening Starseeds. I wanted to join other authors writing personal stories, and Radhaa Publishing House made it simple and empowering to share from my heart in a real, raw way. This team of conscious, awesome Starseeds encourages a revolution to Awaken other Starseeds worldwide!" - **Stasia, Utah**

This is an opportunity to STEP OUT, SPEAK OUR TRUTHS. This is our time, an obligation to share and support others that live in fear and question their soul paths, their soul journey. **- Breda, Canada**

At **Radhaa Publishing House,** we are highly involved in the entire process and work personally with the authors to navigate authorship challenges.

Our authors are heart-centered, soul-driven, and ready to manifest their legacy. We acknowledge the courage and strength it takes to step out into the public eye, and our team is here to support you all the way.

Creating a book is a tedious process and requires persistence, patience, and perspective. There are many moving parts of the book that need attention, and our team knows how to work hard to ensure we can come through with flying colors for the final date of our release.

Step into your voice and be heard now! When you become a contributing writer or an author of Radhaa Publishing House, you empower yourself in a way you may have never experienced before. That's what our authors tell us. Claim your author power now!

"Be that change you wanted to be in our world!"

If you have a compelling story to share with the world, dream of being a published author, and wish to be a part of the Radhaa Publishing family, reach out to us.

"No other publishing company offers you in-house support the way that Radhaa Publishing House does. Your legacy awaits!"

* * *

To find out more information about how to Join us,

Become an Author or See our Upcoming Books, please visit our Website at:

www.RadhaaPublishingHouse.com
Email: RadhaaPublishing@gmail.com

&

To Order a Signed Copies of our Books, visit our

Online Store: https://radhaanilia.net/shop/
Email us: RadhaaPublishing@gmail.com

Thank you!

You Make a Difference When You Support Our Holistic Books!

Published Books:

Awakening Starseeds:
Shattering Illusions, Vol.1
Awakening Starseeds:
Stories Beyond The Stargate, Vol. 2
Awakening Starseeds:
Dreaming into the Future, Vol. 3
Pillars of Light:
Stories of Goddess Activations™
Energy Healing & Soul Medicine
Quan Yin Goddess Activations™
Healing Workbook
Infinite Cosmic Records:
Sacred Doorways to Healing
& Remembering
Stories of the Goddess:
Divine Feminine Frequency Keepers
Dolphin Oddssey

Forthcoming Books:

Poems From the Heart
Mahárliká: In Search of Identity
Embracing Aloha
Time is Promised to No One
Honor Time
Conductor of Time
Memoirs of a Galactic Goddess - 2nd Edition
Descendants of Lemuria: Memoir

WHERE YOU CAN FIND RADHAA PUBLISHING HOUSE BOOKS:

Amazon.com
Barnes and Noble
Target
Walmart
Powell Books
Radhaa Publishing House
&
Get your Signed Copy at Radhaa Publishing House

Email: RadhaaPublishing@gmail.com
Thank you for your support!

TO OUR READERS:

Dear Readers,

Thank you for taking the time to read this book. You are not just a reader but warmly welcomed on this journey of self-discovery and empowerment as you explore the DOLPHIN ODYSSEY. Take this invitation as a call to action as you unlock the wisdom contained within this book. It's a time for remembrance, reconnecting with your true essence, and recognizing your place in the grand tapestry of life. Embrace your love for spiritual books like this and know, with certainty, the paramount importance of your role in shaping the future of our World is valuable. Support us and Together we RISE!

With Love, *RPH Team*

"If you like our book DOLPHIN ODYSSEY
Please leave us a review.
REVIEW this Book ONLINE at: Amazon.com.

We can't do it without your loving support!
Many Blessings and Thank You!
With Love & Gratitude,
Radhaa Publishing House"